Time and the River Flowing:

GRAND CANYON

by FRANÇOIS LEYDET

EDITED BY DAVID BROWER

SIERRA CLUB · BALLANTINE BOOKS

We are grateful for permission to reprint excerpts from the following:

Atheneum Publishers, New York: *The Firmament of Time*, by Loren Eiseley, copyright 1960 by Loren Eiseley.

California Academy of Sciences, San Francisco: "Requiem for a Canyon," *Pacific Discovery*, May-June 1964.

E. P. Dutton & Co., Inc., New York: *Ring of Bright Water*, by Gavin Maxwell, © copyright 1960 by Gavin Maxwell.

Holt, Rinehart and Winston, Inc., New York: *The Colorado*, by Frank Waters, copyright 1946.

Houghton Mifflin Company, Boston: *Beyond the Hundreth Meridian*, by Wallace Stegner, copyright 1954. *Silent Spring*, by Rachel Carson, copyright 1962.

Alfred A. Knopf, Inc., New York: *This Is Dinosaur . . .* , edited by Wallace Stegner, copyright 1955.

J. B. Lippincott Co., Philadelphia and New York: *The Peninsula*, by Louise Dickinson Rich, copyright 1958.

Oxford University Press, Inc., New York: *A Sand County Almanac and Sketches Here and There*, by Aldo Leopold, copyright 1949.

Random House, Inc., New York: (on pages 54, 150)*The Immense Journey*, by Loren Eiseley, © copyright 1957.

William Sloane Associates, New York: *The Voice of the Desert*, by Joseph Wood Krutch, copyright 1956; *Grand Canyon*, by Joseph Wood Krutch, copyright 1957, 1958 by Joseph Wood Krutch. Reprinted by permission of William Morrow and Company, Inc., Publishers.

The University of New Mexico Press, Albuquerque: *The House at Otowi Bridge*, by Peggy Pond Church, copyright 1962.

Addresses: SIERRA CLUB
1050 Mills Tower, San Francisco, Calif. 94104
233 Massachusetts Ave., Washington, D.C. 20002
15 E. 53 St., New York, N. Y. 10022
6 Langley Street, London, W.C.1, England

BALLANTINE BOOKS
101 Fifth Avenue, New York, N. Y. 10003

FOREWORD

*The canyon is at least two things besides spectacle. It is a biological unit and the
most revealing single page of earth's history anywhere open on the face of the globe.*
JOSEPH WOOD KRUTCH

Time, two billion years of it, laid down the stone of what Powell called the Plateau Province. Within that plateau would be some of the most colorful and dramatic natural sculpture man ever saw.

Time and the river flowing—the Colorado River through the milleniums—carved deep, created the great canyon, and is still shaping it.

Standing on its rim in 1903, Theodore Roosevelt said: "In the Grand Canyon, Arizona has a natural wonder which, so far as I know, is in kind absolutely unparalleled. . . . I want to ask you to do one thing in connection with it in your own interest and in the interest of the country. . . . Leave it as it is. You cannot improve on it. The ages have been at work on it, and man can only mar it."

Upstream and unmarred was the exquisite beauty of Glen Canyon. Most of it was destroyed early in 1963 when the U.S. Bureau of Reclamation closed a dam that was not necessary for this century and perhaps would never have been necessary. Now the same bureau has proposed to build dams in Grand Canyon itself as part of its Pacific Southwest Water Plan—to end the living river's flowing for all this civilization's time.

The dams the bureau plans to build in Marble Gorge and at Bridge Canyon, within the Grand Canyon proper, would destroy not only the living river but also the unique life forms that through the ages have come to depend upon the river's life. The major part of the canyon walls would still be there, but the pulsing heart of the place would be stopped. A chain of destructive forces would be begun in what by law was set apart as part of the National Park System, to be preserved unimpaired for all America's future.

And needlessly. Looked at hard, these dams are nothing more than hydroelectric power devices to produce electricity and dollars from its sale to pay for projects that ought to be financed by less costly means. The dams would make no water available that is not available already. Indeed, they would waste enough to supply a major city and impair the quality of the too little that is left: water already too saline is made more so by evaporation, to the peril of downstream users, especially of neighbors in Mexico. All this on a river that already has more dams than it has water to fill them.

Grand Canyon will go the way Glen Canyon did as *The Place No One Knew* pointed out, unless enough people begin to feel uneasy about the current interpretation of what progress consists of—unless they are willing to ask if progress has really served good purpose if it wipes out so many of the things that make life worthwhile, unless they are willing to question whether growth and progress are the same and whether the gross national product is really the measure of the good life. Like the earlier book, *Time and the River Flowing* has a moral: True progress does not deny to the people their inalienable right to be informed and to choose. In Glen Canyon the people never knew what the choices were. Now, in Grand Canyon, where there is wildness that can remain part of our civilization instead of fall victim to it, the people need to know before a bureau's elite decide to wipe out what no men can replace. The Sierra Club has no better purpose than to try to let people know in time. In Glen Canyon we failed. There could hardly be a costlier peacetime mistake—unless there were a repetition of it in Grand Canyon.

* * *

When the Sierra Club undertook the book on Glen Canyon, there was almost no literature on the subject. John Wesley Powell treated it briefly in his accounts of his Colorado River exploration, and we used much of what he said. We borrowed heavily from writing about the Colorado in general, using excerpts that worked well with Eliot Porter's color photographs and augmented his own splendid chapter, "The Living Canyon." And we drew upon what Wallace Stegner described as "a chorus of voices *for* the wilderness." That book was too late to help save Glen Canyon. The conservationists' last chance vanished when the alliance against the Colorado River Storage Project dissolved in ignorance, false assumption, and in naïveté—ignorance about the beauty of the place, false assumption about the necessity of the dam, and futile hope that the Bureau of Reclamation would honor an agreement not to impair the National Park System. The book could only be a beautiful requiem. No one will ever again see the canyon as it was.

With Grand Canyon it is different. The world knows it already. Millions of people have seen it and photographed it from the rims. Thousands have taken the trails into it and have learned about the canyon's depth at the quarter-way point—when they reach the bottom and must climb the vertical mile back out. Hundreds have followed Powell's example and, profiting from his mistakes, have run the Colorado down through its grandest canyon. A handful have run up it. At least one man has walked it, although not at river level.

The literature is impressive—about the place itself, about the meaning of the park, about the meaning of the Colorado to an arid land, about the life which that land supports. None of the literature, however, seemed sufficient in itself to combine with photographs and get to the heart of the crucial issue: what is important, in Grand Canyon, about the living river? We knew it was important for a number of vital reasons, but saw no easy way to demonstrate it. After all, wasn't the river running clear now and then, thanks to Glen Canyon dam? In a canyon more than a mile deep, what difference would a blue lake make, so small in those depths? Wouldn't it let tourists go up and down the canyon in power boats? And wasn't the Colorado River already dead, killed by Glen Canyon dam? Would modest releases of water from that dam ever revive it? As Wallace Stegner pointed out, every side canyon whose flood debris used to be swept away by the spring flood would now dump boulders and snags into the reduced river. Wouldn't this create permanent barriers and turn the river into a series of pools? In summation, what harm would it do to change the blue pools of an already dead river to a continuous blue pool, or even to divert the dead river into a dark tunnel between its fluctuating reservoirs, then squeeze the power out of it with one more hydropower installation, and by this device put more water on a thirsty land?

There must be a book to help people understand, to involve them. What should it say? Some inkling came to me in two significantly different trips up the head of Lake Mead. The first of these was in spring, 1962. The river was still free in Glen Canyon but Lake Mead was nevertheless heavily drawn down. For all that, a man who really knew how to navigate through mud could get into the canyon beyond the Pierce Ferry silt dump, where the river drowns and inters itself at its contact with the reservoir.

Bill Belknap, of Boulder City, knew the regimen of Lake Mead mud extremely well. Sensing where the channel was and scraping bottom only once, he took the Sierra Club's editor, Bruce Kilgore, and me some thirty miles above Pierce Ferry to Spencer Canyon. We spent the night at Spencer's bar. Not far from the reservoir's high-water mark in Spencer canyon—beyond the jungle in which tamarisks and sand bars had alternately lived and died in their impenetrable symbiosis—we discovered that there could still persist in that remote side canyon most of the elements needed for a renewing wilderness experience. The next day we had pushed up still farther, past Separation Canyon, past Bridge Canyon damsite, into an inner sanctum revealed when the Colorado cut into the Vishnu schist, the oldest rock yet exposed on earth. There was something almost sacred about what the river, with grain upon grain in its turbid load, had relentlessly chiseled and rounded and polished in that old obdurate stone. We went just a little bit farther up the river, up into the middle of the lowest of the Colorado's remaining rapids, which were still safely above the waters of Lake Mead that had long since drowned Separation Rapid. Bill Belknap could have taken us on up into the canyon but we didn't have the time. So he found a convenient standing wave, turned around it, and headed back downriver. Not, however, until we had felt the river's pulse. There it was, the big river, the sum of its thousand tributaries, boiling, whirling, and above all, alive.

Two Easters later my wife and two of my children were at Spencer Canyon, lucky to make it: perhaps no one but Mack Miller, of Temple Bar, could have found a way through the massive silt barrier now denying lower Grand Canyon to all lesser river people than he. Lake Mead was really down now. The effort to fill Lake Powell left far too little water for Mead. Twice Mr. Miller told us he couldn't make it. Then he tried once more. He took us up to the edge of the silt dump, eased his jet boat into it here and there, looked hard at the water, then backed far enough away to charge full speed across the murky reservoir surface. He aimed at where he thought the channel was and guessed right.

We were now speeding up through a strange, sad world in which the Colorado was running again, the first time since the closing of Hoover Dam obliterated its channel. Philip Hyde's photograph on page 121 suggests the kind of place it was. The world was mud, its surface cracking, oozing, and tottering into the opaque river, which had resumed its interrupted assignment and was seeking but not finding the sculptured shores the river had taken a lifetime to create.

There wasn't much flow. Very little water was being released from Glen Canyon's gates and not much was being added from the Paria or the Little Colorado. Yet we saw no blue pools. The water totally lacked the clarity a new Bureau of Reclamation film "Clear Water on the Colorado," had tried bravely to sell the public. The water was just about as muddy as it had ever been. We knew that 4,000 cubic feet of Colorado per second, or even the 8,000 to 12,000 which the releases might one day average out, was much less than the 100,000 or more an uncontrolled flood might bring were there no Glen Canyon dam. Separation Canyon and Spencer Canyon showed us what would happen. Flash floods would still come down the side canyons and had. The old bars were gone—the pleasant reservoir beaches where you could nose your boat in, plop ashore, camp in the tamarisks, and explore upstream. Only an untamed Colorado could build those bars back. A tamed Colorado could not do it.

Mack Miller took us up as far as the lowest virgin rapid. In spite of the extremely low flow, the river was still working; it still had its tools and its pulse. Living things came as close to the river banks as the floods had ever let them. The river swirled and murmured and sang, whirlpooled in the sucks and exhaled bubbles in the boils, foamed over the rocks and ground at them along the edges, deposited a cool softness alongside where herons could track it, floated the ducks that had paced us upstream, watered the willows, continued to chisel at what might lie below the schist, stood in throbbing waves alongside out boat, splashed us, excited us—and was vital throughout. While it lived, so would the canyon.

If we could see how alive the river was from that brief experience, François Leydet and his river-expert friends and photographers were learning far more. They were two hundred miles upstream at the time, riding the river down. We are grateful for what they saw and for what the book can therefore reveal. We are grateful too to those who weren't there but whose wisdom we have borrowed and have used as counterpoint—especially to Loren Eiseley, Joseph Wood Krutch, and Wallace Stegner.

We could testify that the river was now badly injured, but far from the dead stream Wallace Stegner once feared it might be. He would have seen that even a vestige of the Colorado is a force to be reckoned with. All along, he has understood the river as few men are likely to. One of his finest contributions has been his book, *Beyond the Hundredth Meridian*. In it he has important things to say about two conflicting forces in the arid lands. One was represented by the vision of Powell, who wanted science to serve government; a government so served could have preserved the best of this country. The other force came from the pervasive illusions of the overoptimistic arid-lands promoter, William Gilpin—illusions such as seem now to inspire the Bureau of Reclamation's attempts to destroy the river by overextending man's dependence upon it. Mr. Stegner's book and Bernard DeVoto's introduction to it are essential to an understanding of the conflict over the Colorado.

*   *   *

In a sense, *Time and the River Flowing* is a continuation of *The Place No One Knew*. Each book tells about the same extraordinary river and its greatest canyons, both fully deserving national-park protection, even though there was not yet vision enough to provide it. Each book draws heavily upon perceptive interpretation by many of America's best writers of what these canyons mean to the world —what Glen Canyon could have meant and what Grand Canyon can always mean. Both books tell of the massive inflexibility and compulsive engineering that lost one canyon forever and seem determined to lose the other. Both books make the plea that this generation do better for all other generations than to let the Bureau of Reclamation carry out its present plans to destroy what is most important in Grand Canyon. The two books reinforce each other, this one reiterating just enough of the Glen Canyon story to underline the tragedy it would be to let the Bureau of Reclamation repeat its mistake—not out of evil intent or incompetence, but from adamantly following a course of action that reveres engineering values and technology and ignores man's soul and sense of wonder.

Let me illustrate. Last summer I was speaking with a former United States Commissioner of Reclamation who had promoted Colorado River development with zeal for many years, who had claimed in public that his bureau liked "to push rivers around," who had spoken disdainfully of opposition by "conservationists in their air-conditioned caves," and who in retirement was trying to help other countries get on with their dam building. He was talking enthusiastically of one especially massive project. "What kind of country would the reservoir inundate?" I asked him. "Nothing but a mess of mountains," he replied.

The Sierra Club has consistently tried to oppose blind progress and to support the kind of values this reclamation commissioner was unable to perceive in a particular mess of mountains. The club is rarely qualified to support a particular engineering solution in river development but does favor what Edward Higbee calls "preventive engineering." Accordingly, in the Columbia River Basin the club has supported a major dam at either the Paradise or Knowles sites because adequate development there could end the threat of upstream dams that would encroach on a national park, on a wilderness area, and on lands of high scenic-resource values that should be dedicated.

The club takes no part in the controversy over allocation of waters of the Colorado River. The club opposed water development that would serve San Francisco, the city of its birth, at the cost of destroying an important part of Yosemite National Park; the club opposes dams threatening parklands on the Colorado just as intensely— except that there are more and more people concerned about the less and less there is to preserve. The club avoids the struggle between private and public power. (There is probably virtue in having both, each to watch the other.)

Neither in this struggle nor in any other does the club feel omniscient. The club leadership went through painful confusion in the Hetch Hetchy dam struggle at the turn of the century, a battle which John Muir and the club lost, as did national park visitors from there on out. The confusion was renewed in the late 'forties when the then club president persuaded the club's directors and the leaders of many major conservation organizations to approve construction of a high Bridge Canyon dam in Grand Canyon providing several conditions were first met: "prior action on construction of Glen Canyon and Coconino dams for silt control; prior amendment of the Grand Canyon National Park Act eliminating secretarial authority to permit reclamation projects within the park; prior legislative action disapproving the Kanab project; prior incorporation of Grand Canyon National Monument into Grand Canyon National Park together with certain boundary adjustments; limitation of the high water level below the junction of Tapeats Creek; and prior commitment to maintain the reservoir at a stable level."

By the following year it was seen that the proponents of Bridge Canyon dam were unwilling to accept the proposed restrictions, so the club directors voted unanimously to oppose construction of any dam within Grand Canyon National Monument.

There was momentary confusion again in the battle for Dinosaur National Monument when one club officer suggested that construction of Echo Park dam within the monument could be blocked best by permitting the construction of Split Mountain dam, also within the same monument but downstream. None of the other directors concurred, and opposition to the entire Colorado River Storage Project continued until the Bureau of Reclamation had made an agreement that was written into law: no project dam or reservoir would lie within any national park or monument and Rainbow Bridge National Monument would be protected from the reservoir behind Glen Canyon dam. At that time too few club leaders knew what was at stake in Glen Canyon—that it deserved full protection as a national park and that a dam in it would be extremely destructive and wholly unnecessary as long as Lake Mead was capable of adequately controlling the Colorado River. Had Glen Canyon been known, and had relevant hydrological data been released, there would today be no Glen Canyon dam. The conservationist force in America could have blocked it. The confusion is not over yet. There are still a few conservationists who think that the only way to keep the Bureau of Reclamation from building an unnecessary dam in Bridge Canyon, violating the national park and monument, is to permit the Bureau to build an unnecessary dam at Marble Gorge, which is technically outside the park but would violate it nonetheless. This book demonstrates the magnitude of the violation.

* * *

Man must disrupt a great part of the planet in order to sustain himself in his present numbers and, reserving judgment about when enough population is enough, the club is in favor of man. It is also in favor of man's being intelligent enough to do better with the ninety-five per cent of the American earth he has already disrupted before he covets the unmanipulated five per cent. The club believes that Grand Canyon National Park and Grand Canyon National Monument should be extended to protect the integrity of the Grand Canyon between Lee's Ferry and the Grand Wash Cliffs, or that this area should be protected by other suitable means that would preserve unimpaired this outstanding scenic part of the river. The club opposes any further dams or diversions in this stretch.

In the course of seeking out the kind of conservationist support that saved Dinosaur National Monument and could, if continued, have saved Glen Canyon, I asked several leading conservationists how we could get around a most troublesome obstacle, the Reclamation Bureau's technique of drafting and (or) signing replies to protests about its activities, no matter to whom in the administration they were addressed.

Dr. Ira N. Gabrielson, President of the Wildlife Management Institute and certainly one of America's foremost conservationists, responded this way:

"The only answer . . . that might work would be to have a board of review composed of eminent scientists who should not be connected with any government bureau either directly or indirectly.

"The big problem with Reclamation as with the Army Engineers and to a lesser extent also with other agencies is that they are the ones who do the planning, who carry out the plan, and who are the final judges as to whether it is a good plan. I am and always have been against this type of setup, but it is a very popular one with Congress. It makes it easier for pork barrel projects when there is enough political pressure behind them.

"I have no illusions but that we are in for a hell of a scrap on this southwest water project. If we lose in the effort to protect the Grand Canyon National Park, I would begin to wonder if we could ever protect any park from blatant commercialism of any kind."

This kind of battle is in the history of every great place that has been preserved. Not just the ancient history, either. In Grand Canyon, as in the other park and wilderness reserves, the battle must be renewed each time someone of great enterprise conspires to reduce wilderness to something else and something less.

*   *   *

In my own role in the steps that produced this book I should like to thank especially François Leydet for doing the impossible and Martin Litton for making the impossible feasible; I also owe thanks to all the people they are thankful to. I am grateful as well to Russell Butcher, John Gregg, David Hales, Bruce Kilgore, my wife Anne and my son Kenneth, who helped comb the literature and the proof; to the club's publications committee members and directors who had faith; to my secretaries, Anne Chamberlain and Hasse Bunnelle, who kept my other conservation work sorted out while the rest of this was going on; to the authors and publishers of other works, excerpts from which have given our own text and photographs extra meaning; to the conservationists who will read this and care.

The most reassuring part of the whole effort to publish the book was the wealth of material we found about the wilderness idea—the *national park* idea, if we go back to the concept that underlay the first great parks and that has been a unique American contribution toward harmony between man and the natural world. We hope that the testimony of the text, combined with the photographers' powers of observation, will serve lasting purpose by in some way stepping up the pace with which mankind preserves what is left of the world's irreplaceables.

DAVID BROWER

New York City
October 17, 1964

FOREWORD TO THE PAPERBACK EDITION

The nearly four years that have ensued since *Time and the River Flowing* first appeared have brought some good news in the battle to save the Grand Canyon. Thanks to an awakened public, and to the presentation before Congress, President Johnson, and Secretary of the Interior Stewart Udall of data that had not been made available before, a new approach has been made to the solution of water problems in the Pacific Southwest and to the nation as a whole —an approach that does not involve the sacrifice of any part of the Grand Canyon. Proposals for a Central Arizona Project financed without Grand Canyon dams have been passed by the United States Senate and House of Representatives. Leaders in both houses and in the Administration have indicated support for the enlargement of Grand Canyon National Park to help insure that the Canyon will always serve its highest purpose—that it will be preserved as a great natural place for all the world to enjoy in perpetuity.

We feel confident that this book helped let the public know what the danger was—our own edition and the Book-of-the-Month Club edition. We think that the full-page advertisements in principal newspapers, although they may have displeased the Internal Revenue Service with the Sierra Club, served a good public purpose that we will continue to try to serve. We know that truth will out, and that when several government agencies that are keepers of the expertise are not allowed to speak freely, people will speak freely in their stead; we will not forget the major contribution, for example, made by three M.I.T. graduates, in nuclear engineering, economics, and mathematics, who in the course of their testimony in cooperation with the Sierra Club forced the Bureau of Reclamation to rethink.

But no one may quite relax as long as there is a Colorado River, running sometimes wild and almost free, in an unspoiled Grand Canyon. To leave it as it is, as Theodore Roosevelt urged, is to tempt those who would change it. And as Joseph W. Penfold of the Izaak Walton League said when he was twitting one of his Reclamation friends, some engineers are just like beaver: they can't stand the sight of running water. We hope that the wide audience of this edition will watch out for these engineers, and will help establish and secure from them a long overdue greater Grand Canyon National Park.

D. B.

London, August 5, 1968

ACKNOWLEDGMENTS

It is both a pleasure and a perplexity to an author to give credit to those individuals and institutions without whose help his book would not have been born. The pleasure is obvious. But the perplexity arises from the need to draw a line between those persons whose aid contributed directly to the book and the many others whose contributions may have been more tangential. If I were to list all the latter, I should begin with my late and much-missed friend, Paul Ramey, with John Lord King and Theo King, with John B. Barnes, Dr. Benjamin Robinson, Dr. William Atchley . . . and could end up with an author's preface nearly as long as the book itself.

Even if I narrow the list down to those whose help was essential to the actual production of the book, I would hardly do justice to their efforts by merely listing their names—and yet space allows me to do little more than that. I can only trust they will appreciate that this brief notice is not the measure of my gratitude.

First of all, my thanks go to those who helped with the research of the book, either by supplying me with essential source material, or by giving me the benefit of their expert knowledge: Martin Litton—whose inspirational assistance throughout the project went well beyond the call of duty or friendship—Ansel and Virginia Adams, Joseph Wood Krutch, Otis R. Marston, Russell D. Butcher, Alexander Hildebrand, Daniel B. Luten, Robert W. Jasperson, and Francis P. Farquhar. Francis Farquhar was particularly kind in placing at my disposal his extensive personal library on the Colorado River, and I must add that I found most useful his critical bibliography, *The Colorado River & The Grand Canyon*.

Then there were the many at and around the Grand Canyon who helped make my stay there one of the most rewarding experiences of my life. My thanks go particularly to J. Harvey Butchart, who gave me invaluable advice about the Canyon's trails, and who with his wife, Roma, offered me many times the hospitality of their home in Flagstaff; to the National Park Service and its officers at Grand Canyon National Park: Superintendent John McLaughlin and his successor, Howard B. Stricklin; Chief Park Ranger A. Lynn Coffin; Chief Park Naturalist Merrill D. Beal, whose office was open to me at all times and who introduced me to the fascinating collections of fossils and zoölogical specimens at the Visitors' Center; his Administrative Assistant Louise M. Hinchliffe, who was ever helpful to me in my research at the Visitors Center library; D. B. McHenry and Vernon Ruesch; and John Riffey, Custodian of Grand Canyon National Monument, interesting guide and delightful host.

I owe an inestimable debt of gratitude to P. T. and Susie Reilly, who did the advance planning and logistical preparation for the three-week river trip through the Grand Canyon which proved to be so essential to the preparation of this book. Pat's knowledge of the river, and Martin Litton's, were invaluable during the trip itself. But the coöperation of every member of the party— Philip and Ardis Hyde, William C. Jones, Dr. Joseph G. Hall, Clyde Childress, Carl Yost, and Patience Leydet— was essential to making it possible as well as a pleasure. Others who were most helpful during the course of the trip, without themselves being a party to it, were William Belknap, Jr., of Boulder City, Nevada, and Chief Ranger James W. Packard, of Lake Mead National Recreation Area, who alerted us to the closing of the gates at Glen Canyon Dam and kept track by plane of our subsequent dash down the river.

The finished manuscript was painstakingly reviewed by P. T. Reilly, Martin Litton, Otis Marston, Wallace Stegner, and Russell Butcher, and is a better product for their numerous and much-valued suggestions and corrections. The text contains a number of quotations from works by other authors, who said certain things better than I could have said them myself. To them, and to their publishers, I am grateful for permission to quote.

My thanks go also to the photographers — Ansel Adams, David R. Brower, Clyde Childress, Joseph Hall, Philip Hyde, Katie Lee, Richard Norgaard, P. T. Reilly, and Clyde Thomas—whose magnificent photographs illustrate this book; to cartographer James W. Cutter, who drew the endpaper map, and Peter Slavinskis, who did the final work on it; to my editor, David Brower, who gave me constant support and encouragement and who put the final product together with his well-known artistry; and to the Publications Committee of the Sierra Club, for the advance enabling me to devote a year to this project.

There is one person without whose steadfast faith and help this book would not have been done; who relieved me of innumerable small tasks connected with my research; who was a cheerful companion on the boat trip and a good sport after the upset in the rapid; who aided me in my writing with constructive criticism; who uncomplainingly performed the chore of typing the final draft; and to whom I dedicate this book as a token of my gratitude. That person is Patience, my wife.   F. L.

CONTENTS

SEVENTY SEVEN COLOR PHOTOGRAPHS

PHILIP HYDE: *Yucca blooms, Toroweap overlook*

1. Toroweap

THE AFTERNOON was well advanced, and the late spring sun had lost some of its fire. A scattered flotilla of small flat-keeled clouds cruised slowly across the sky. The wind was from the west, warm and insistent, a clean desert wind that spoke of sage and of sand and of sun-baked rock. It stirred the needles of the pinyon pines, and rocked the tall stalks of the yuccas, with their spires of creamy blooms.

To the south, a dust devil scurried restlessly across the broad shelf of the Esplanade. And beyond, out of the haze, loomed the Canyon's upper cliffs, stretching from east to west in a continuous gray-buff scarp, two thousand feet high. These cliffs' northern counterparts reared behind me and to my left, jutting out into promontories which revealed their profile: a sheer drop from the rim for half their height, then a long concave curve levelling off into the Esplanade. Directly behind me these cliffs described a sharp bend beyond which, unseen from where I stood, they receded to the north. The wide, level U of the Toroweap Valley down which I had driven intervened between them and the volcanic mass of the Pine Mountains. These in turn were partly hidden behind the perfect cone of Vulcan's Throne, not far to my right.

The vast sweep of this view, the architectural perfection of its individual forms, provided spectacle enough. Yet as I walked away from the car toward the south I knew that the climax still lay ahead. I also knew what it would be—the three-thousand-foot chasm of the Canyon's inner gorge. From a hundred feet or so away I could see the upper portion of the farther wall. But even with such foreknowledge I was unprepared for the impact of this abyss. The angle of sight revealed little more as I approached Toroweap overlook, until the very last step. Then, all at once, the solid ground at my feet dissolved into air. Drawn irresistibly as if by the force of gravity, my gaze plummeted down the cataract of red cliffs across the way until it came to rest on the Colorado River, a narrow ribbon of brown in the blue-tinted depths. Leaning forward as far as I dared, I studied the precipice at my feet: first a perfectly sheer cliff of red sandstone, then, several hundred feet down, a steep, narrow talus slope, then again nothingness all the way to a sandy beach by the river.

I retreated a step, sat down on the smooth sandstone ledge, and carefully slid forward till my feet hung over the brink. These movements were rather timid, and though there was no one within miles, I felt rather silly. But I was acutely conscious of the three thousand feet of air that separated the soles of my boots from the river below. Such a perspective is not common in our civilized lives, except perhaps when viewed through the window of an airliner. And accustomed to the security of glass or steel railings when gazing into a void we tend to glimpse, in their absence, the portals of eternity. I thought then of the little man I had met at Bright Angel Lodge, on the south rim of Grand Canyon National Park. He was standing out on the terrace, camera in hand, and seemed to be executing a hesitant sarabande. He would slowly take a step or two forward, toward the parapet some thirty feet away, then move back to his starting point. He would look at the low wall for a few seconds, advance a yard or two towards it, and retreat again. My curiosity aroused, I engaged him in conversation. We exchanged a few banalities, then, his eyes still fixed on the parapet, he said, "You know, I just can't bring myself to look down over that wall. Could you take a picture of the Canyon for me?" I gladly complied, thinking as I did that courage takes many forms. He had not had the nerve to walk up to the edge, but he'd had the greater courage to confess his fright.

Now, as I sat perched with my feet dangling out into space, the memory of that encounter faded along with my uneasiness. What mattered was the Now, the overwhelming present. Only this was real, these colors, these shapes, these rocks, this air. Once again, as so often in the past months, the Grand Canyon was casting its spell, gradually seeping into every cranny of my consciousness. It can, if you will let it, act on you like a drug, and alter the nature of reality. The uncertainties of the future, the exigencies of the present, the perplexities of the past become such stuff as dreams are made on. The past is there, yes—but it is the past of long-dead species, the past of vanished seas and of mountains long since crumbled into dust.

The dust devil had hurried on and dissolved in the distant haze, and the only movement now visible in the immensity spread before me was that of the white-throated swifts. With alternate strokes of their back-swept wings they hurtled by at incredible speed, with a sound like tearing silk. One would fly straight at the cliff, swerve at the last split second, dive into the gorge, swoop back up with effortless grace. Now and then a pair would mate on the wing, in a marvelous display of coordination and singleness of purpose. Theirs was the only sentient life in sight. Nowhere in all this vastness was there a single sign of man, or even a hint that he had ever existed. No need for warnings here, such as are posted along the rim near Bright Angel Lodge, not to throw rocks over the edge lest they strike someone on the trail below. Yielding to a temptation which is strong in most of us, I stood up, walked over to a good-sized slab, tilted it with difficulty and toppled it off the brink. Then I counted, eight, nine, ten, eleven seconds till I heard the sharp crack of its impact, followed by a clatter like machinegun fire as its fragments cascaded down the talus slope below. Had I remembered the formula for the acceleration of gravity I could have calculated the distance of the fall, but I had forgotten it, which did not matter as my senses told me more than any figure could. And so the experiment did not prove very much, except perhaps that the child dies hard.

It was tempting, too, to try to hurl a stone over to the opposite rim, which looked easy enough to reach. But this, I knew, was an optical illusion. Those lumps of vegetation over there which looked at first glance like sagebrush were pinyons and junipers—smallish trees to be sure, but trees nonetheless. That farther rim which appeared so close was in fact a half mile away, and the gorge at this point was almost as wide as it was deep. In terms of accessibility that rim was even more remote, for though the swifts could cross that half mile I could not. On the other side of Vulcan's Throne a trail of sorts, marked here and there with ducks, ran down to the river. One hiker who had scrambled down the precipitous lava slide had written of the Toroweap Trail that she wondered which would reach the bottom first, the topography or she. But once at the river's edge there would be no way across: the trail ends just above a rapid, called Lava Falls by some and Vulcan Rapid by others but regarded by all as the fiercest on the Colorado. And even suppose, for a moment, the river had been fordable. There still remained the formidable problem of scaling that avalanche of cliffs and taluses on the other side. The half mile facing me must surely be one of the longest in the world. For the quickest route over to those scattered pines and junipers was by way of St. George,

Utah; Las Vegas and Boulder City, Nevada; Hoover Dam; Kingman and Peach Springs, Arizona—a total of 450 miles across desert and range, 160 of them dirt roads and trails.

Dusk had settled on the river and its banks, and the shadow of oncoming night crept up the far wall. The evening light washed across the Esplanade to the south and broke against the face of the Canyon's upper cliffs. Their details now appeared in sharp focus. Brightly lit capes contrasted with shadowed bays, and twenty miles to the east Sinyala Butte, which had been almost indistinguishable in the flat afternoon light, now stood boldly detached.

The swifts were relinquishing the air to the bats, slower flyers but even more agile in their sudden swerves and swoops. The wind was dying down, and in the crepuscular hush time itself seemed to have paused. The whole vast scene was utterly serene, with that serenity peculiar to the greater works of nature. This quality, though so palpable, I found hard to define. The vastness of the scale may have contributed to it. The harmony of the colors—the gold-streaked blue of the evening sky, the purple of the shadows, the reds and yellows of cliffs and rocks, the muted greens of the semi-desert plants—was doubtless part of it too. So was the loneliness, and the silence—a silence disturbed only by a faint murmur from the river, the voice of a small rapid exhausted by the distance. But mostly, I thought, it was the *rightness* of it all. There was nothing haphazard, nothing obtrusive or out of place in this landscape. It had contrasts, but no conflicts; diversity without chaos. Mere chance had not dictated the shapes of these great cliffs, nor had the river which had cut them set a capricious course. Obeying a few simple laws, using a few simple tools, nature had worked unhurried through a myriad of yesteryears and had come up with this. The result was inevitable, it was right—and it was sublime. The real miracle of the Grand Canyon was that nature had needed no miracles in its making.

No miracle but one, I corrected myself. It had happened long ago, more than a billion years. Unobserved and unrecorded in the warm surface waters of sun-bedazzled seas, the miracle of life had transfigured this earth. It was low life at first, mere blobs of undifferentiated protoplasm. But it had possibilities of improvement and elaboration. By and by, after a few million centuries, some marine organisms sported limey shells or skeletons. When they died, their bodies drifted down and settled in the sea-bottom ooze. This gentle rain of small calcareous corpses, continuous over millions of years, piled up great depths of carbonate of lime; these in turn gradually hardened into limestone. Those several hundred feet of limestone cliffs below me, those further hundreds of feet of limestone in the Canyon's upper walls, were the mass graves of countless little lives. Without life there could have been no limestone. And without the limestone, the Grand Canyon would have been much less grand.

What difference did it make, you might ask, to know that this cliff was made of limestone, that talus made of shale? Or that gray-tailed squirrels with tufted ears of the south rim had white-tailed cousins on the north? What did such knowledge have to do with seeing the beauty of the Canyon? A great deal, I had found. At first the Canyon's effect, although awesome enough, had been somewhat stupefying. It was only slowly, as I learned something of its logic, that I began to glimpse the real splendor of the Canyon. It was the difference between hearing the Eroica for the first and the fiftieth time. In the *Tertiary History of the Grand Canyon District*, published more than eighty years ago but still perhaps the greatest of all Grand Canyon books, geologist Clarence Dutton wrote:

"The Grand Canyon of the Colorado is a great innovation in modern ideas of scenery, and in our conceptions of the grandeur, beauty, and power of nature. As with all great innovations it is not to be comprehended in a day or a week, nor even in a month. . . . The lover of nature, whose perceptions have been trained in the Alps, in Italy, Germany, or New England, in the Appalachians or Cordilleras, in Scotland or Colorado, would enter this strange region with a shock, and dwell there for a time with a sense of oppression, and perhaps with horror . . . But time would bring a gradual change. Some day he would suddenly become conscious that outlines which at first seemed grotesque are full of dignity; that magnitudes which had added enormity to coarseness have become replete with strength and even majesty; that colors which had been esteemed unrefined, immodest, and glaring, are as expressive, tender, changeful, and capacious of effects as any others. Great innovations, whether in art or literature, in science or in nature, seldom take the world by storm. They must be understood before they can be estimated, and must be cultivated before they can be understood."

I had cultivated the Canyon during the past months and been well rewarded for my time, though my knowledge was still fragmentary and my understanding incomplete. To really know the Canyon, a man would need to be geologist, paleontologist, botanist, mammalogist, ornithologist, herpetologist, entomologist, climatologist, hydrologist, archaeologist, and historian all rolled up into one, and have more than one lifetime at his disposal. Such men as geologist Dr. Edwin McKee and former chief park naturalist Louis Schellbach had spent years at the Grand Canyon and were still learning about it when they left.

My knowledge would have been even more disjointed except for one thing. About a week before, I had completed a three weeks' boat trip through the length of Grand Canyon from Lee's Ferry to Lake Mead. This had been much more than a sporting expedition, although there had been thrills enough. It had been more than an exercise in outdoorsmanship, although the wilderness had been our home. It had been more than a sightseeing excursion, although we had seen many stretches of the river accessible only by boat.

A month earlier, the Grand Canyon still had been a kaleidoscope of sights and impressions and a potpourri of facts—fossil clams and tourist crowds, Indian ruins and projected dams, a snowstorm in the ponderosas and a sunrise at Desert View, a pioneer's journal and a coyote's bark in the night. Somehow, the gradual journey down the river made a whole of all these parts. Geology and topography, climate and living things, the hopes and hardships of men long dead and the boondoggles of today's bureaucrats, all fell into place, bound together by the river's connecting thread. And I was left with a new appreciation of the majestic unity of the Grand Canyon, a unity which mocked the artificial boundaries of park and national forest, monument and reservation and recreation area.

The sun was setting now, over the shoulder of Vulcan's Throne, and I took a last long look at the river before repairing to my camp. The light down there was fading fast, but a little above the rapid's white water I could still recognize the tamarisk-fringed beach where we had made camp, ten days or so before. I could almost see the three little red-and-white boats beached side by side, hear the lapping of the water against their sterns, smell the smoke of the driftwood fire. And as I lingered over that memory the lines of Edith Warner echoed in my mind:

"This is the day when life and
the world seem to be standing still—
only time and the river flowing past the mesas. . ."

The Walls

The Grand Canyon of the Colorado is a great innovation in modern ideas of scenery, and in our conceptions of the grandeur, beauty, and power of nature. As with all great innovations it is not to be comprehended in a day or a week, nor even in a month. It must be dwelt upon and studied, and the study must comprise the slow acquisition of the meaning and spirit of that marvelous scenery which characterizes the Plateau Country, and of which the great chasm is the superlative manifestation. . . . The lover of nature, whose perceptions have been trained in the Alps, in Italy, Germany, or New England, in the Appalachians or Cordilleras, in Scotland or Colorado, would enter this strange region with a shock, and dwell there for a time with a sense of oppression, and perhaps with horror. . . . But time would bring a gradual change. Some day he would suddenly become conscious that outlines which at first seemed harsh and trivial have grace and meaning; that forms which seemed grotesque are full of dignity; that magnitudes which had added enormity to coarseness have become replete with strength and even majesty; that colors which had been esteemed unrefined, immodest, and glaring, are as expressive, tender, changeful, and capacious of effects as any others. Great innovations, whether in art or literature, in science or in nature, seldom take the world by storm. They must be understood before they can be estimated, and must be cultivated before they can be understood.

It is so with the Grand Canyon.

. . . There are in the world valleys which are longer and a few which are deeper. There are valleys flanked by summits loftier than the palisades of the Kaibab. Still the Grand Canyon is the sublimest thing on earth. It is so not alone by virtue of its magnitudes, but by virtue of the whole — its *ensemble*.

. . . As a great cathedral is an immense development of the rudimentary idea involved in the four walls and roof of a cabin, so is the chasm an expansion of the simple type of drainage channels peculiar to the Plateau Country. To the conception of its vast proportions must be added some notion of its intricate plan, the nobility of its architecture, its colossal buttes, its wealth of ornamentation, the splendor . . .

Clarence E. Dutton

PHILIP HYDE: *Cliff detail, Toroweap overlook*

The observer who, unfamiliar with plateau scenery, stands for the first time upon the brink of the inner gorge, is almost sure to view his surroundings with commingled feelings of disappointment and perplexity. The fame of the chasm of the Colorado is great; but so indefinite and meager have been the descriptions of it that the imagination is left to its own devices in framing a mental conception of it. And such subjective pictures are of course wide of the truth. When he first visits it the preconceived notion is at once dissipated and the mind is slow to receive a new one. The creations of his own fancy no doubt are clothed with a vague grandeur and beauty, but not with the grandeur and beauty of Nature. When the reality is before him the impression bears some analogy to that produced upon the visitor who for the first time enters St. Peter's Church at Rome. He expected to be profoundly awe-struck by the unexampled dimensions, and to feel exalted by the beauty of its proportions and decoration. He forgets that the human mind itself is of small capacity and receives its impressions slowly, by labored processes of comparison. So, too, at the brink of the chasm, there comes at first a feeling of disappointment; it does not seem so grand as we expected. At length we strive to make comparisons. The river is clearly defined below, but it looks about large enough to turn a village grist-mill; yet we know it is a stream three or four hundred feet wide. Its surface looks as motionless as a lake seen from a distant mountain-top. We know it is a rushing torrent. The ear is strained to hear the roar of its waters and catches it faintly at intervals as the eddying breezes waft it upwards; but the sound seems exhausted by the distance. We perceive dimly a mottling of light and shadow upon the surface of the stream, and the flecks move with a barely perceptible cloud-like motion. They are the fields of white foam lashed up at the foot of some cataract and sailing swiftly onward.

. . . And now the real magnitudes begin to unfold themselves, and as the attention is held firmly the mind grows restive under the increasing burden. Every time the eye ranges up or down its face it seems more distant and more vast. At length we recoil, overburdened with the perceptions already attained and yet half vexed at the inadequacy of our faculties to comprehend more.

CLARENCE E. DUTTON

What is there in it that exerts so universal an appeal? For one thing, it contains every shape known to man. Lofty peaks, whole mountains rise out of its depths. There are vast plateaus, flat-topped mesas, high buttes and monoliths. And all these are carved in the semblance of pyramids, temples, castles; of pinnacles, spires, fluted columns and towers; porticoes and abutments, bridges and arches, terraces, balconies, balustrades. They are solid and fragile, bare and covered with latticework and delicate carving. It is a stage that seems expressly built to contain in perpetuity appropriate sets for every dynasty, every religion, every legend and myth-drama that man has known—a vast universal depository, as it were, of mankind's structural and architectural heritage.

FRANK WATERS

PHILIP HYDE: *Upriver from Toroweap overlook, 3,000 feet down to Mile 177*

The magnitude of the chasm, however, is by no means the most impressive element of its character; nor is the inner gorge the most impressive of its constituent parts. The thoughtful mind is far more deeply moved by the splendor and grace of Nature's architecture. Forms so new to the culture of civilized races and so strongly contrasted with those which have been the ideals of thirty generations of white men cannot indeed be appreciated after the study of a single hour or day. The first conception of them may not be a pleasing one. They may seem merely abnormal, curious, and even grotesque. But he who fancies that Nature has exhausted her wealth of beauty in other lands strangely underestimates her versatility and power.

CLARENCE E. DUTTON

I looked across the ten miles to the opposite rim, down the successive terraces to the inner gorge at whose invisible bottom the great river still runs after having cut through a mile of stone, and then at the wall of an opposite promontory on my own side. I checked where I could the dividing lines between the successive formations of the geological ages—the Permian limestone on which I sat, the hundreds of feet of sandstone below it, the great Redwall of the Carboniferous age, the resisting plateau of Cambrian sediments, and finally the black wall of Archean schist. I made, in other words, a brief attempt at adjustment to the world of time as well as of space. But for the moment I was less interested in what the Canyon had been than in what it is at this moment and has been able to remain. It is not often that twentieth-century man has so much space to himself.

JOSEPH WOOD KRUTCH

ANSEL ADAMS: Detail, spur of Grand Canyon wall
  Coconino sandstone, overlying Hermit shale (top red slope),
  Supai formation (cliffs and taluses), Redwall limestone (vertical red cliff),
  Muav limestone, and Bright Angel shale of Tonto Platform

Below is the canyon, through which the Colorado runs. We can trace its course for miles, and at points catch glimpses of the river. . . . Away to the west are lines of cliff and ledges of rock —not such ledges as you may have seen where the quarryman splits his blocks, but ledges from which the gods might quarry mountains, that, rolled out on the plain below, would stand a lofty range; and not such cliffs as you may have seen where the swallow builds its nest, but cliffs where the soaring eagle is lost to view ere he reaches the summit. . . . Wherever we look there is but a wilderness of rocks; deep gorges, where the rivers are lost below cliffs and towers and pinnacles; and ten thousand strangely carved forms in every direction; and beyond them, mountains blending with the clouds.

JOHN WESLEY POWELL

The inner gorge, as we sit upon its brink, is indeed a mighty spectacle; but as we withdraw a little it fades out of view, and, strangely enough, the sublimity of the scene is not very greatly impaired. It is, after all, a mere detail, and the outer chasm is the all-engrossing feature. On either side its palisades stretch away to the horizon. Their fronts wander in and out, here throwing out a gable, there receding into a chamber, or gaping widely to admit the entrance of a lateral chasm. The profile is ever the same. It has nothing in common with the formless, chaotic crags, which are only big and rough, but is definite, graceful, architectural, and systematic. The width of the space inclosed between the upper walls is one of the most essential elements of the grandeur. It varies from five to six miles. If it were narrower the effect would be impaired; nor could it be much wider without diluting and weakening the general effect. This proportion seems quite just.

CLARENCE E. DUTTON

PHILIP HYDE: Downriver from near Powell Monument, South Rim

Those who are familiar with western scenery have, no doubt, been impressed with the peculiar character of its haze —or atmosphere, in the artistic sense of the word — and have noted its more prominent qualities. When the air is free from common smoke it has a pale blue color which is quite unlike the neutral gray of the east. It is always apparently more dense when we look towards the sun than when we look away from it, and this difference in the two directions, respectively, is a maximum near sunrise and sunset. This property is universal, but its peculiarities in the Plateau Province become conspicuous when the strong rich colors of the rocks are seen through it. The very air is then visible. We see it, palpably, as a tenuous fluid, and the rocks beyond it do not appear to be colored blue as they do in other regions, but reveal themselves clothed in colors of their own. The Grand Canyon is ever full of this haze. It fills it to the brim. Its apparent density, as elsewhere, is varied according to the direction in which it is viewed and the position of the sun; but it seems also to be denser and more concentrated than elsewhere. This is really a delusion arising from the fact that the enormous magnitude of the chasm and of its component masses dwarfs the distances; we are really looking through miles of atmosphere under the impression that they are only so many furlongs. This apparent concentration of haze, however, greatly intensifies all the beautiful or mysterious optical defects which are dependent upon the intervention of the atmosphere.

CLARENCE E. DUTTON

HILIP HYDE: *Upriver from Powell Monument, South Rim*

In its own aloof, almost contemptuous, way it is nevertheless extraordinarily beautiful—nature's ultimate achievement in that Southwestern Style which surprisingly executes great monolithic forms, sometimes sculptural and sometimes architectural, in bright, multihued sandstone. About the style there is nothing to suggest the charm of the landscape which welcomes man; instead, there is only the grandeur of something powerfully alien, indifferent, and enduring, as though it had been made to please the eye and perhaps even to soothe the spirit of some creature older, as well as less transitory, than he. . . .

JOSEPH WOOD KRUTCH

The walls now are more than a mile in height—a vertical distance difficult to appreciate. Stand on the south steps of the Treasury building in Washington and look down Pennsylvania Avenue to the Capitol; measure this distance overhead, and imagine cliffs to extend to that altitude, and you will understand what is meant; or stand at Canal Street in New York and look up Broadway to Grace Church, and you have about the distance; or stand at Lake Street bridge in Chicago and look down to the Central Depot, and you have it again.

A thousand feet of this is up through granite crags; then steep slopes and perpendicular cliffs rise one above another to the summit. The gorge is black and narrow below, red and gray and flaring above, with crags and angular projections on the walls, which, cut in many places by side canyons, seem to be a vast wilderness of rocks. Down in these grand, gloomy depths we glide, ever listening . . .

JOHN WESLEY POWELL

T. REILLY: *Southeast to Sinyala Butte from Boysag Point,*
Havasu Canyon upper right

. . . Another common and mistaken idea is that the chasm is pervaded by a deep, solemn gloom. The truth is almost the reverse. In the depths of the inner gorge there is a suggestion of gloom, but even in the narrower portions there is seldom less than sixty degrees of sky from crest to crest, and a hundred and sixty along the track of the river. In the outer chasm the scene is unusually bright. . . .

. . . Between the cataracts the stream outspreads to great width and rushes swiftly by. It is almost always turbid, and generally is charged with a heavy load of sand and silt. On the lowest talus near the brink may be seen lines of high-water mark, some as high as fifty or sixty feet above the ordinary summer stages. Within those stages the rocks are ground and polished, carved into strange shapes, and worn by pot-holes from the scouring of the current. All of the boulders are rounded and ground away, or have become carious and crumbly by the chemical reactions of air and water. All things plainly reveal the powerful effects of corrosion acting with extreme energy. We do not wonder at it now. The impetuous rush of the waters charged with sharp sand even at the lower stages is amply suggestive, and the mind is at a loss to conceive what must be the power of the river when its volume is many times multiplied.

CLARENCE E. DUTTON

The largest river west of the mountains and yet the least known. There are miles upon miles of mesas stretching upward from the stream that no feet have ever trodden, and that possess not a vestige of life of any kind. And along its banks the same tale is told. You float for days and meet with no traces of humanity. When they do appear it is but to emphasize the solitude.

JOHN C. VAN DYKE

CLYDE CHILDRESS: Limestone walls, downriver from Havasu

We are now ready to start on our way down the Great Unknown. Our boats, tied to a common stake, are chafing each other, as they are tossed by the fretful river....

We are three quarters of a mile in the depths of the earth, and the great river shrinks into insignificance, as it dashes its angry waves against the walls and cliffs, that rise to the world above; they are but puny ripples, and we but pigmies, running up and down the sands, or lost among the boulders.

We have an unknown distance yet to run; an unknown river yet to explore. What falls there are, we know not; what rocks beset the channel, we know not; what walls rise over the river, we know not. Ah, well! we may conjecture many things. The men talk as cheerfully as ever; jests are bandied about freely this morning; but to me the cheer is somber and the jests are ghastly.

JOHN WESLEY POWELL

How many more generations will pass before it will have become nearly impossible to be alone even for an hour, to see anywhere nature as she is without man's improvements upon her? How long will it be before —what is perhaps worse yet —there is no quietness anywhere, no escape from the rumble and the crash, the clank and the screech which seem to be the inevitable accompaniment of technology? Whatever man does or produces, noise seems to be an unavoidable by-product. Perhaps he can, as he now tends to believe, do anything. But he cannot do it quietly.

Perhaps when the time comes that there is no more silence and no more aloneness, there will also be no longer anyone who wants to be alone.

JOSEPH WOOD KRUTCH

PHILIP HYDE: Camp below Toroweap, Mile 177,
where Bridge Canyon reservoir would be 300 feet deep

2. Lee's Ferry

From THE San Francisco Bay Area and from Los Angeles, from Nevada and the Sierra, from north and south of the Grand Canyon, we had converged the last week end of April on Cliff Dwellers Lodge, a small group of low buildings faced with native stone, nestled against the foot of the aptly named Vermilion Cliffs and with the desert for its front yard. There were nine of us in the party: photographer Philip Hyde and his wife, Ardis; Martin Litton, a director of the Sierra Club; William Jones, a painter and photographer and some-time National Parks seasonal ranger, who would row one of the boats; Dr. Joseph Hall, of San Francisco State College, a biologist who had been conducting an eco-logical study of the Kaibab squirrels; P. T. Reilly, on leave from Lockheed Aircraft and our admiral of the fleet, and his wife Susie; my wife Patience and I. The Reillys and Martin Litton were experienced canyoneers —they had totaled more fast water miles between them than the entire sum of miles run through the Grand Canyon up to 1900. William Jones and Philip Hyde had traversed the Grand Canyon once apiece. For the rest of us, this trip was a journey into the unknown.

A strong current of excitement, anticipation, and re-spect for the challenge of the river united us all, even the veterans of the run—for a blasé Colorado boatman is as unlikely a type as a blasé matador. And though all of us were there for a definite purpose—photographic, literary, or scientific—I think to some extent we also shared, con-sciously or unconsciously, something of the feelings Pat Reilly expressed to me in a letter written after the trip: "Over the years many people have asked me why I keep going back to Grand Canyon. This cannot be answered in a few words. Man cannot rationalize himself into a state where he does not have to cope with the natural physical environment. Not yet. Man can lose his ability even to survive in the natural environment by lack of contact with it. I like to keep my hand in and be sure that even though I utilize asphalt and the gasoline engine, I haven't sold myself to them."

On the eve of our departure the day broke clear and warm, and after an unhurried breakfast we took off for Lee's Ferry with the boats in tow. The eight miles of paved highway between the Lodge and Navajo bridge ran northeastward along the base of the Vermilion Cliffs. To the right of the road stretched a broad expanse of al-most featureless desert, a slightly undulating plateau of bare rock and sparse sagebrush extending far to the south and to the foot of the red Echo Cliffs to the east. The plateau's western limit was the long swell of the East Kaibab monocline, edge of the forested Kaibab Plateau which forms the north rim in Grand Canyon National Park.

There was a marvelous expansiveness to this high, wide landscape, and I resented the confinement of the automobile. The cliffs which rimmed the sky were several thousand feet high, but separated by miles of open desert they were impressive without being oppres-sive. Perhaps the very featurelessness of the Marble Plat-form, as this plateau is called—not a tree in sight, not a salient knoll or butte—contributed to the overall sense of spaciousness. Here and there, the road crossed a steep-sided wash, but these trenches revealed themselves only when one reached their brink. The biggest trench of the lot, into which all others drained, was just as incon-spicuous. Though it paralleled the road about two miles away, there was no hint that anything as prodigious as the Marble Gorge of the Colorado interrupted the smooth sweep of the terrain between us and the Echo Cliffs. But such is the nature of this country, and it adds much to its drama. A mountain chain announces itself from scores of miles away, but these canyons of the plateau country, these inverted mountains, seem to lie low in wait for you and explode on you when you least expect it. This effect reaches its climax in Grand Canyon National Park. Whether you drive in from the north or the south, you approach for miles through a thick ever-green forest, and all you can see ahead is more trees. Then, suddenly the forest ends and so do any precon-ceived notions you might have had about the Grand Canyon, as you find yourself without warning looking down into this unbelievable gulf.

Just before the highway curved down to Navajo Bridge, we turned off to the left onto a dirt road. Trailing clouds of dust we skirted the base of a butte shaped like Rheims Cathedral but several times larger, ran past great boulders eroded into odd toadstool shapes, crossed a small creek rather ambitiously named the Paria River, and drew up at the head of the ramp sloping down into the Colorado River.

In the 443 miles between Hite, Utah and Pierce Ferry on Lake Mead, Lee's Ferry was one of the few spots on the river where the walls were low and broken enough to allow automobiles to reach its banks. The far side was a low cliff, and in its face we could see the dugway or trail up which pioneers' wagons had been hauled after being ferried across the river. On the near bank, a jungle of low willows and tamarisks grew along the water's edge, the willows just leafing out and adorned with yellow catkins. Wide and shallow, the river swept by with a swishing sound. It was running low, about 11,000 cubic feet per second, and comparatively clear. Still, in the few miles between Glen Canyon Dam and here the river had picked up some silt, and swirls of brown marbled its green waters.

A few fishermen were about, watching our activities with curiosity. We eased the boats off their trailers into the water at the new launching ramp and rowed them 50 yards or so upstream to the old launch site, where we tied them to willows and tamarisks on the shore. Then began the tedious work of making final adjustments to the trim of the boats, threading handlines around their hulls, wrapping and securing leather around new oars, sorting all the food into three piles, and stowing it aboard. Pat Reilly's boat, the *Susie Too*, and Martin Litton's, the *Portola*, were outsized McKenzie river dories, flat-hulled 16-footers with a sharp upward rake to their pointed sterns and bows. With sealed decks fore and aft and water-tight compartments built into their cockpits they were practically unsinkable, and the compartments permitted the storage of food and gear out of the boatman's and passengers' way. The third boat, a regular 15-foot McKenzie dory, was brand new and there had been no time to fit it with bulkheads or compartments. Everything aboard it that must be kept dry had to be carried in watertight rubber bags and tied down, and plastic bottles were secured in the forepeak to give the craft extra flotation in case of a swamping or an upset.

But it was difficult in this place to imagine such emergencies. There was nothing ominous about the Canyon at Lee's Ferry. Open to the sun, it seemed to drowse in the afternoon warmth. Beaver had been here, and a large willow near our mooring had been partly chewed through by their chisel-like teeth. Yellow warblers and rufous-crowned sparrows flitted about the thicket of willow and tamarisk, and violet-green swallows sped low over the water. From across the river came the song of the canyon wren, a sweet-toned cascade of chromatic appoggiaturas. This was a peaceful place and I rather envied Bill Jones, who had been picked to camp by the boats overnight. As we walked up to the cars, our work done for the day, he was stretched out flat in the big willow's shade, a picture of drowsy contentment.

Just beyond the cars stood a small, low building so inconspicuous that until then I had paid it no attention. But this, Pat Reilly pointed out, was Lee's old fort. Suddenly interested, I walked over and studied it. It was only a two-room structure with small windows, built of local rock laid together without mortar. It was in need of repair, though the timber and brush roof still looked fairly watertight. In a similar building not far away, on August 15, 1872, two highly unusual men had had dinner together.

John Doyle Lee and Major John Wesley Powell already had made names for themselves, each in his own way. Lee's exploit would take him before a firing squad five years later; Powell's had won him quick fame and his star was still rising. But a prudent man might have thought Lee the safer actuarial risk as Powell was due the next day to resume his second descent through the Grand Canyon. There was nothing dramatic in their meeting, nothing to suggest that either man made an extraordinary impression on the other. Frederick Dellenbaugh, then a boy of 17 who was accompanying Powell, noted only that "Lee was most cordial" and that they enjoyed "the first watermelon of the season for dessert." Still, this meeting was interesting in retrospect because both men were playing an important role in the exploration and opening up of the country's last big wilderness.

By the mid-eighteen hundreds, three centuries had passed since the first white man had looked into the Grand Canyon, yet the Grand Canyon country was still a blank on the map. Disappointment, frustration, hardship, and defeat had been the common fate of the men who had sought to penetrate it.

The first explorers of the region were the Spaniards. In 1536, Alvar Nuñez, Cabeza de Vaca, and three companions straggled into Mexico City after a nine-years' tramp across the continent from Florida, the sole survivors of Pánfilo de Narváez' abortive attempt to colonize the peninsula. Along the way they had heard tales from the Indians of great cities across the desert far to the north of New Spain. Surely, the Spaniards thought, these must be the Seven Cities of Cibola, paved with gold and sparkling with emeralds and rubies. In 1539 Fray Marcos de Niza was sent to find the Seven Cities, taking along as a guide the Negro slave Esteban, who had been one of de Vaca's companions. Esteban went ahead to scout, and for a few glorious days he was received as a god in the Indian villages through which he passed, his every whim accommodated by an adoring retinue of Indian girls. But his hour of triumph was brief: he was captured by the "Cibolans" and died transpierced by their arrows. Fray Marcos returned to New Spain, but not, as he reported to Viceroy Antonio de Mendoza, before he had looked down from a hill upon the first city of Cibola, "a very beautiful place, bigger than Mexico City."

On the strength of this description, Francisco Vásquez de Coronado was despatched a year later at the head of a brilliant army of several hundred horse and infantry with orders to conquer the Seven Cities. And conquer they did, but their prizes were the lowly pueblos of the Zuñi, built of mud and stone, instead of the richest cities in the world. The province of Tusayán, as the Spaniards called the Hopi country, was reached by Pedro de Tovar, but the Hopi villages turned out to be distressingly similar to the Zuñi's.

As a financial venture—and every man of the expedition had invested in it out of his own pocket—the Coronado foray was a bust. As a geographical exploration it was a brilliant success—and its climax was yet to come. The Hopi had talked of a great river to the west, which Coronado correctly guessed should flow to the Gulf of California. Don García López de Cárdenas was sent out with a dozen horsemen to find this river. Picking up some Hopi guides along the way, Cárdenas traveled west until halted by the most stupendous natural phenomenon ever to have been seen by Christian eyes. Unfortunately Cárdenas left us no description of his emotions or those of his men as they stood on the south rim of the Grand Canyon. We can only infer their amazement. They tried for days to find a way down to the river, and three of the party got a third of the way down before they were forced to turn back. On their return, they reported incredulously that pinnacles which from the top had seemed no larger than a man were in fact taller than the greatest tower in Seville.

Did they see any beauty in the Grand Canyon? Probably not. Nature in the raw was not rated very highly in the aesthetics of the time. "Horrid" and "awful" were adjectives usually applied to untamed wilderness. It had to be tidied up, improved by man before it could be thought beautiful — a view widely held even today. Rather, Cárdenas and his men probably regarded the impenetrable canyon as just another frustration on an altogether lamentable journey. But though they could

not know it this frustration spared them a greater one: had they succeeded in crossing the Grand Canyon they would have found no golden cities but only scattered bands of Paiute Indians whose standard of living was a great deal lower yet than that of the Zuñi or Hopi pueblo dwellers.

If the Grand Canyon country made no lasting impression on the Spaniards, the Spaniards made even less of an impression on it. The zenith of their influence was the years 1600–1680, when Franciscan missionaries lived among the Hopi and tried to convert them to Christianity. But the conversions, as it turned out, didn't take. By 1680 the Hopi had had enough of plunder, murder, and rape by Spanish soldiers, and joining in a general revolt by the Pueblos, they martyred the priests. They reverted at once to the worship of their Kachina gods, in which they have happily persisted to this day, and never again was a Spaniard allowed entrance into a Hopi town. In 1776 Fray Francisco Tomás Hermenegildo Garcés, an extraordinary man who combined a sincere love for the Indians, tireless missionary zeal, and the constitution of an Apache, undertook a 2500-mile muleback voyage from mission San Xavier del Bac near Tucson to southern California and across the whole breadth of northern Arizona. Along the way he visited the Havasupai in their idyllic retreat in Havasu Canyon, a tributary of Grand Canyon, and so charmed them that they sought to detain him with the offer of a wife. He graciously declined the offer, climbed out of Havasu Canyon, skirted the south rim of Grand Canyon (the first man to do so since Cárdenas) and called at the Hopi villages. But the Hopi remained adamant in their hispanophobia, and Garcés had to ride away from the site of his first rebuff.

For the next three quarters of a century the Grand Canyon's isolation remained practically undisturbed. The era of the fur trade came and went, a forty-year boom during which every stream west of the Rockies was cleared of beaver and, as Weldon Heald puts it, "bear, deer, raccoon, marten and all other animals unlucky enough to have fur coats were slaughtered by the millions." An incredibly hardy and self-sufficient breed of men, the trappers ventured deep into the canyon country. Some of the mountain men—Kit Carson, Jim Baker, "Old Bill" Williams, Antoine Leroux, Jedediah Smith—saw the Grand Canyon or its immediate environs. But they added nothing to public knowledge of the geography of the area. They talked little and wrote less. The only one to leave a written record, in fact, was James Ohio Pattie, who in 1826 followed the rim of the Grand Canyon for thirteen days without succeeding in reaching the Colorado. But his *Personal Narrative*, published in 1831, was so vague in its descriptions that one cannot tell from it whether he was on the north rim or the south. The voyage and the scenery were "horrid" from start to finish, and one can feel Pattie's relief when at last he arrived "where the river emerges from the horrid mountains, which so cage it up as to deprive all human beings of the ability to descend to its banks and make use of its water." Three centuries earlier, Cárdenas must have felt much the same.

The Conquistadores had brushed by the Grand Canyon looking for cities of gold—and the cities had proved a mirage. The Padres had come in search of souls to save, and the souls had eluded them. The Mountain Men had penetrated the canyons seeking a fortune in furs, and their quest was self-limiting since it involved the extermination of the fur-bearers. The moral seemed clear: this was not white man's country. And such was the verdict of the leader of the first official U.S. Government expedition to visit the Grand Canyon. In 1857, Lieutenant Joseph C. Ives was ordered by the War Department to explore the "Colorado River of the West" and "to ascertain [its] navigability" for steamboats. This part of his mission was a waste of the taxpayers' money, since river pilot Johnson already had taken a steamboat well above Black Canyon, where Hoover Dam now stands. And as it turned out, Ives got his smaller *Explorer* —which had been built in Philadelphia and shipped in sections through Panama—only to Black Canyon, whence he continued in a skiff to the mouth of Las Vegas Wash, then came back to Beal's Crossing and proceeded overland toward the northeast. But this last part of his exploration made history.

The Ives party descended Diamond Creek to the Colorado, becoming the first white men to reach the river in the Grand Canyon. They climbed down into Havasu Canyon, almost to the home of the Havasupai. They worked along the south rim until thirst forced them south in a long detour to the Hopi Indian country. Ives had along with him Dr. John Strong Newberry, an able geologist who wrote the first accurate account of the canyons of the Colorado, and whose work was to influence Powell's. He also had with him as expedition artist Baron von Egloffstein, who drew the first—and thoroughly *in*accurate—pictures of the Grand Canyon, pictures described by bibliographer Francis Farquhar as "invariably deplorable," by Wallace Stegner as "portraits of the artist's dismay," and by Joseph Wood Krutch as "a surrealist's interpretation of claustrophobia." But what is perhaps best remembered about

this expedition is Ives' unlucky prophecy: "Ours has been the first, and will doubtless be the last party of whites to visit this profitless locality. It seems intended by nature that the Colorado river, along the greater portion of its lonely and majestic way, shall be forever unvisited and undisturbed."

The Grand Canyon today is one of the most visited places on the face of this earth—more than 1,500,000 persons came to Grand Canyon National Park in 1963. Ives would have had to be clairvoyant to foresee the changes in transportation that would make the Canyon so easily accessible, or the rapid conquest of the wilderness that would make such remnants as the Grand Canyon rarities to be prized. But even in his day white men were closing in on the canyon country. In 1847, the Mormons' great westward trek ended when Brigham Young and his followers climbed down the Wasatch Mountains into the valley of Utah's Great Salt Lake. Although remembered principally for their exuberant polygamy, these Mormons were remarkable in other ways also. They seemed to be endowed with superhuman energy, and they built cities, planted farms and opened up new territory with astonishing rapidity. In the 1850's and 1860's they settled the area to the north of the Grand Canyon. From Salt Lake City, the Vatican of the Church of Jesus Christ of Latter-Day Saints, there issued a steady stream of instructions for further settlements and explorations. One of the most trusted agents of the Church was Jacob Hamblin, the "Leatherstockings of the Southwest." Hamblin crossed and crisscrossed the canyon country, keeping an eye on the settlements, making friends among the Indians, a number of whose languages he reputedly learned. In 1863, he made the first complete circuit of the Grand Canyon, starting from St. George, finding a new and better crossing of the Colorado at Pearce's Ferry (today's Pierce Ferry), traversing the Hualpai Indians' country, visiting the Havasupai and the Hopi before returning home via Ute Ford in Glen Canyon.

John Lee was also one of the leaders of the Saints. "He had all the typical qualities to a greater than common degree," writes Joseph Wood Krutch in *Grand Canyon.* "Though barely literate, his advice in both spiritual and practical matters was sought and followed. The desperately ill sent for him to ride miles in the middle of the night that he might lay his blessed hands upon them. If they died, it was God's will; if they recovered, it was another demonstration of his superhuman powers. Nor did he fail to prosper as the righteous should. He had many wives and many farms. In fact, it was his usual practice to set up each new wife on a new farm which she managed between the regular visits of inspection he paid to each."

Unfortunately for Lee, he became involved in one of the more gruesome incidents in the history of the old West. On September 11, 1857, a wagon train of immigrants from Arkansas and Missouri was waylaid at Mountain Meadows, Utah, by Indians and Mormons. The adults (115 or 123 of them, depending on which report one reads) were slaughtered to the last man or woman, and seventeen infants distributed among Mormon families. From one point of view, this was just retribution: The Mormons themselves had been the victims in the East of massacres at the hands of the "gentiles," massacres which had spurred their hegira to the West. And they could only resent the invasion by their enemies of the territory they had painfully carved for themselves out of the wilderness. Just what part Lee played in the action remains in dispute. According to Dellenbaugh, "Lee gave me his own version of the Mountain Meadows Massacre claiming that he really had nothing to do with it and had tried to stop it, and when he could not do so he went to his house and cried. The Pai Utes ever after called him Naguts or Crybaby." On November 7, 1874, U. S. Deputy Marshal William Stokes caught up with Lee at Panguitch, Utah, and brought him to Beaver, Utah, to stand trial. At his trials (the first, July 23-August 5, 1875, ended in a hung jury; the second began September 14, 1876) Lee refused to save his life by incriminating the Church authorities, although in several interviews and letters he described himself as a scapegoat. And indeed, he alone of the persons implicated was found guilty as charged by an all-Mormon jury on September 20, 1876. On March 23, 1877, seated on his coffin at the site of the massacre, he was executed by a firing squad.

But in the twenty years between the alleged crime and its punishment, Lee continued to make himself useful. In 1872, he settled with two of his wives, Emma and Rachel, at the mouth of the Paria, a place Emma named Lonely Dell. He built a house, planted some fields which he irrigated with water from the Paria, and according to Dellenbaugh, "had his farm in fairly good order with crops growing" by the time the Powell party came to call. At some time in the same year Lee started to operate his ferry across the Colorado at that point, and until his arrest two years later, he continued to transport companies of Mormon immigrants on their way to settle northern Arizona. After his execution, the ferry was operated for some years by Emma, then was taken over successively by the Mormon Church and by Coconino county, Arizona, until in 1929 it was rendered obsolete by the present Navajo Bridge.

But for all their industry, their zest for exploration, and their colonizing zeal, the Mormons did not advance much beyond the fringes of the Grand Canyon. On the maps of the day the Canyon and its environs were still a blank space labeled "unexplored." In just three years, 1869–1872, one man succeeded in dispelling the Canyon's major mysteries, geographical and geological. That man, whose adventures we will follow shortly, was Lee's dinner guest of August 15, 1872, Major John Wesley Powell.

Lee's Lonely Dell may not be lonely too much longer. As we drove away that afternoon and headed back for Cliff Dwellers Lodge, we passed an incongruous sight. On the broad gravel bench northwest of the mouth of the Pària, bright red fire hydrants stood regularly spaced along concrete street curbs, and a picnic-camp loop had been almost completed, with modernistic curved windbreaks, picnic tables, barbecue grills, and rest rooms. They're really jumping the gun, I thought. Marble Gorge Dam had yet to be authorized, let alone built—yet here they were already erecting facilities for hypothetical speedboat owners and water skiers who might some day seek recreation on Marble Gorge Reservoir. This was absurd, but it was frightening too—frightening evidence of the arrogance of the dam builders, of their confidence that the public could be duped indefinitely by juggled figures proving the necessity of dams that would be obsolete before they could be paid for. But that is another story which we will postpone for the moment.

What would they call the reservoir if Marble Dam were built, I wondered? Lake Lee? I could imagine Lee's surprise if he could see the fire hydrants by the Paria, or hear the snarl of speedboats echo from the cliffs rimming his Lonely Dell. But then, as he sat on his coffin that day at Mountain Meadows, he would have been surprised had he been told that one day a polished granite monument would be erected to his memory near the west end of Navajo Bridge, and that the inscription would say:

"To . . . John Doyle Lee, who, with superhuman effort and in the face of almost insurmountable obstacles, maintained this ferry which made possible the colonization of Arizona. Frontiersman, trailblazer, builder, a man of great faith, sound judgment, and indomitable courage."

3. Soap Creek

THE OAR blades dipped soundlessly into the smooth, opaque water, traveled a few inches without rippling the surface, lifted back into sight and hovered motionless, dripping gently from their lower edges. Long seconds drifted by as the drip gradually stopped, then the blades glided back for the next slow stroke. In, out, pause. Some bubbles broke the surface a few feet to our right, and kept pace with the boat until the last one burst. Quiet voices floated up to us from the *Susie Too*, a hundred feet ahead. A like distance behind the *Portolá* hung in midstream, neatly framed by the Canyon walls, and appeared immobilized as if in a photograph. We three were in a trance. Now and then Bill Jones went through the motions of rowing, but he put no weight into his strokes and the boat just drifted on at the river's own pace. Drugged by the hot sun and the warm colors of the sky and rocks we sat silent, watching the Canyon's wings slowly glide by.

Except for the brief, booming ride through Badger Creek Rapid after lunch, our first day on the river had been a peaceful one. A few people had waved to us from the bank that morning as our flotilla of bright-colored dories pushed out into the current, and we had waved back, feeling brave and excited. But within minutes, past the small riffle of fast water at the mouth of the Paria, the somnolence of the windless day had seeped into us. Little by little the walls of the Canyon had grown higher, sealing us off from the outside world. An hour and four miles from our departure we had coasted under the silver arch of Navajo Bridge as a car passed nearly five hundred feet overhead, honking a salute. Now, six miles farther, the rims of the gorge loomed a thousand feet high, enclosing a wide band of deep blue sky. One by one the different strata of its walls had risen from river level, soon to be pried upward by the wedge of the next band of rock. We had ticked them off as they appeared: Kaibab limestone, Toroweap formation, Coconino sandstone—the latter surprisingly thin at this point, whereas farther west in the Canyon it forms a great sheer buff-colored cliff some three hundred feet thick. All these strata were now far overhead, and the bottom half of the gorge on either side of the river was a steep talus slope that glowed with the rich red of the Hermit shale.

We were in a straight aisle of the Canyon some two miles long, bearing west-southwest, and there was no shade in sight except that afforded by the feathery tamarisks on the streamside sand bars. At this low level of water these beaches were frequent, some pristine except for wind ripples in their low dunes, some marked with the tracks of the canyon-dwellers. Four pairs of beaver tracks showed clearly on a sandbank to our right. A little farther down, the paw prints of a ring-tailed cat ran along the water's edge. Many of the tamarisks were in bloom, a mist of pastel pink softening the vivid green of the foliage. Here and there, a desert plume caught the sun in a burst of bright yellow. A beautiful little male sparrow hawk wheeled overhead, a flash of speckled blue and rust and cream, and lit among the boulders on the talus to our right. Every few minutes, issuing clear and disembodied from somewhere in the cliffs, came the falling tones of the canyon wren's song.

Directly ahead, a great buff fortress of rock seemed to block the Canyon, and we might have been nearing the head of a narrow lake. But in the sleepy stillness of the hot mid-afternoon we gradually became aware of a new sound. It was almost imperceptible at first, hardly a sound at all but a sort of toneless vibration in the air. It grew in volume as we approached the hidden bend of the river, and began to acquire the characteristic pitch of a major rapid, a booming, deep-throated roar, a pulsing growl that underscored the noise of the waves like an organ pedal point. We rounded the bend, where the river curved to the left and the canyon of Soap Creek cut in from the right, and the roar waxed suddenly in a mighty crescendo. Our eyes were glued ahead, in the direction of the noise, but the rapid itself remained hidden. There was a sharp line from shore to shore, at which the river seemed to end. All we could see beyond the drop were dancing jets of spray—the broken tops of the big waves or haystacks.

"Land on the right," Pat Reilly called from the *Susie Too*, and we all put in above the mouth of Soap Creek, making the boats fast to boulders on the shore. The fan built up by the floods that had washed down the side canyon was beautiful. A mosaic of varicolored rocks ranging in size from pebbles to boulders rimmed a small green reflecting pool, and blue phacelia, delicate orange desert mallow and golden desert plume added touches of bright color to wind-layered sand dunes. But I noted this beauty with only half an eye, being more intent just then on sizing up my first really big rapid. Climbing onto a boulder that jutted out into the stream we stood silently contemplating the fury of the river. Before us was the tongue, a V of smooth water that projected down from the mirror-slick stretch above the head of the rapid. On either side of and below the tongue, all was madness. The river boiled and churned and tumbled and frothed. It exploded into great jagged waves eight to ten feet high that crested and curled back on themselves in perpetual circular motion. Unlike the ocean, where the waves move but the water is stationary, here the water was ever rushing downhill while the wave pattern remained fixed. Between the waves great holes yawned, deep enough for a boat to be lost from sight in them. Here and there the current curled over a barely submerged rock and seemed to plunge straight down to the bottom of the river bed. For two hundred yards or more this turmoil continued until it subsided at last in the tail waves downstream.

Pat Reilly, Martin Litton, and Bill Jones discussed the best route through the rapid. Then Pat Reilly announced his decision: the women would walk downstream to the foot of the rapid, and could take photographs of the boats going through; he would run the rapid first, with Joe Hall aboard; Bill Jones and I would follow, a hundred feet behind; Martin Litton and Phil Hyde would bring up the rear. Below the rapid we would pull in to a beach on the right bank and make camp. Trying to look matter-of-fact I walked back to the boats, untied them and pushed off. Bill Jones rowed out into the current, turned the boat so that he was facing downstream, then let it drift with the flood. Up ahead, Pat Reilly stood on his seat, oars in hand, peering down at the rapid. He sat down, rowed a few strokes to the left to correct his approach, stood and looked again, finally sat down for good and faced the *Susie Too* downstream. There was need for all this caution, for the entrance into the rapid was crucial. Too far on the right side of the tongue and he would crash against a rock—as Martin Litton had done in Badger Creek Rapid earlier; too far to the left and he would tumble into a hole in which he could easily upset.

I watched, tense and expectant, as the *Susie Too* slid down the tongue, reared into the first big wave, plunged into the trough beyond, heaved back up in a big splash of spray. Then I forgot about them, for *our* turn had come. We glided down the tongue, gathering speed with every yard. We were committed—there was no way to turn back or to try a different approach. And oddly enough with that realization my apprehension ceased, giving way to a feeling of aliveness and exhilaration. "Here we go!" Bill Jones shouted as the boat was swept into the first wave, almost standing on its transom. For a split second we perched on its crest like the cap on a mushroom, then we pitched violently down. Bill Jones pulled hard on the starboard oar to turn the bow into a wave; the oarlock pin broke, the oarlock pulled out of the gunwale, Jones lost his balance and almost lost the oar. I made a grab for it and managed to catch it before it went overboard. I tried to slip the lock back into place but the boat was tossing too wildly and I couldn't find the hole. A big wave thundered up out of nowhere, slammed against the port bow; it drenched us and half filled the boat. Bill Jones tried vainly with one oar to head into the waves. I gave up on the oarlock, swung around and started using the oar as a canoe paddle, laughing at myself and thinking, *This won't do much good but it's worth a try.* "Here comes a big one!" Bill Jones bellowed over the roar of the rapid, "head her up, head her up!" It hit us hard, a great pyramid of brown water and spray, and we careened drunkenly over. Before we could tip, a wave hit us from the other side, filling the boat still more but serving to right it. We were wallowing now, almost awash, but luck was with us—we were through the big water and down among the tail waves. Bill Jones grabbed a spare oarlock, slipped it into place, slid the oar into it, and once more could row. I picked up a bucket and began to bail, mixed elation and relief coursing hotly through my veins like a strong shot of whiskey.

An hour or so later we had pulled the boat, now baptized the *Lucky Pierre*, up against the current to where the others were beached; we had spread our wet things out on the sand to dry, had gathered driftwood and flat rocks and lit a cooking fire, and were sitting around it devouring our dinner. The evening was magnificent with the sunset glow slowly fading from the opposite rim of the gorge, but the air grew noticeably chillier as we finished supper, and after clearing away the pots and dishes we built up the fire and huddled around it. With the din of the rapid throbbing in our ears, we reviewed the day's events. We had traveled a little more than eleven miles, had run two rapids, in each of which one of the boats had had trouble—the *Portolá* with that rock in Badger, the *Lucky Pierre* in Soap. In the 268 miles still to go scores of rapids awaited us, many of them as large as

Soap or larger. The Grand Canyon's rapids were really dangerous only for the unwary or unprepared—nearly every drowning had been due to failure by the victim to wear a life jacket, and certainly there were more lives lost in an average decade on the "safe" waters of Lake Mead than had been lost in almost a century on the Colorado through the Grand Canyon. But obviously the river required total respect and total attention to business from those who would brave its angry waters. Granted this respect and attention, it would offer in exchange one of the most exhilarating experiences available on the face of this earth.

William Jones entertained us by reading a page from Major Powell's journal: "We are now ready to start on our way down the Great Unknown. Our boats, tied to a common stake, are chafing each other, as they are tossed by the fretful river. They ride high and buoyant, for their loads are lighter than we could desire. We have but a month's rations remaining. The flour has been resifted through the mosquito-net sieve; the spoiled bacon has been dried, and the worst of it boiled; the few pounds of dried apples have been spread in the sun, and re-shrunken to their normal bulk; the sugar has all melted, and gone on its way down the river; but we have a large sack of coffee. The lighting of the boats has this advantage; they will ride the waves better, and we shall have but little to carry when we make a portage.

"We are three quarters of a mile in the depths of the earth [this described a point down river from us, at the mouth of the Little Colorado], and the great river shrinks into insignificance, as it dashes its angry waves against the walls and cliffs, that rise to the world above; they are but puny ripples, and we but pygmies, running up and down the sands, or lost among the boulders.

"We have an unknown distance yet to run; an unknown river yet to explore. What falls there are, we know not; what walls rise over the river, we know not. Ah, well! we may conjecture many things. The men talk as cheerfully as ever; jests are bandied about freely this morning; but to me the cheer is somber and the jests are ghastly."

As I listened to Powell's words, I thought of the contrast between our situation and his. Decades of experience in western river running had gone into the design of our boats. The Canyon had been traversed at all stages of water and could hold no real surprises for us. Our boatmen were experienced; and Pat Reilly in particular had an amazing memory of every bend in the river, of the idiosyncrasies of every rapid. And our canned food could not spoil.

Powell's boats, on the other hand, could not have been less suitable for the job they were to do. Long, narrow-beamed, and round-hulled, they maneuvered like logs and rolled over as readily. Three of them, built of well-seasoned white oak, double-ribbed with double stem and sternposts, and strengthened by bulkheads at each end, weighed over a thousand pounds each and were a brutal weight to portage. The fourth, shorter and built of white pine, was lighter and more maneuverable but upset as easily. The boats' design, which was Powell's own, testified to his qualifications as a boatman. Powell himself of course could not row—he had lost an arm at the battle of Shiloh. And only two of his nine companions, Jack Sumner and George Bradley, had had any experience with boats. The food consisted of the usual army rations—flour, sugar, beans, dried apples, salt pork, coffee, and tea, to which Powell added a few sides of bacon and some rice. This would be supplemented—or so it was hoped—by fish and game caught as the journey progressed. The rations were the only contributions to the expedition by the government: costs were defrayed by funds obtained from three small Illinois educational institutions, from friends, and from Powell's own pocket.

As for information on what lay ahead, Powell had little and could trust none. Indians cited legends that told of long stretches where the river flowed underground. White frontiersmen, such as James P. Beckwourth, warned of fierce sucks or whirlpools, of waterfalls greater than Niagara. But Powell, who had taught natural science at Illinois Wesleyan University, knew a good deal about geology and had done some exploring of the upper canyons of the Grand River (the name then given to the portion of the Colorado above its confluence with the Green), reasoned that a stream with the cutting power of the silt-laden Colorado was unlikely to plunge over any Niagaras. And so it was with confidence that he pushed off from Green River City, Wyoming, on the morning of May 24, 1869, his boats loaded with ten months' food, summer and winter clothing, guns and ammunition, tools, and scientific instruments including barometers, chronometers, thermometers, and compasses.

Two weeks passed without major mishap. Then, on June 8, the party passed through the Gates of Lodore and entered a gorge with walls three thousand feet high. Rapid followed rapid and several upsets were logged in the course of the day. On the following day one of the big boats, the *No Name*, was dashed to pieces against a rock. Its three occupants narrowly escaped drowning, a quarter of the provisions were lost along with many of the scientific instruments, and a few days later one of the *No Name*'s crew, the Englishman Frank Goodman, left the party overland.

On July 16, Powell and his men reached the junction of the Green and the Grand. By the Major's calculation he had traveled 538 miles already. How many more miles lay ahead he could not know (it was actually 500). But it was reasonable to suppose that the Colorado, with the combined flows of the Grand and the Green, would tumble through fiercer rapids, and cut through deeper gorges than any traversed so far. The food situation was already alarming. In just over two months, eight months' rations had disappeared—most of it in the *No Name*'s disaster or through wetting and spoiling. The men had had little luck so far with hunting and fishing. There were supplies left for eight weeks—if no more were lost to the river.

On July 21 the party started off again. Cataract Canyon, as the Major later named this gorge, proved to be as difficult as expected. The rapids were so hemmed in by boulders that they could not be lined—a process by which the boats were let down along the sides of the big water on lines from shore—but must be portaged, and on an average of four times a day the men had to heave and wrestle the cruelly heavy boats overland around the rapids. On the afternoon of the 31st they reached the mouth of the San Juan, and Powell ordered a halt of several days to make observations. Bradley wrote in his diary: "August 2nd . . . doomed to be here another day, perhaps more than that for Major has been taking observations ever since we came here and seems no nearer done now than when he began. He ought to get the latitude and longitude of every mouth of a river not known before and we are willing to face starvation if necessary to do it but further than that he should not ask us to wait, and he must go on soon or the consequences will be different from what he anticipates. If we could get game or fish we should be all right, but we have not caught a single mess of fish since we left the junction."

On the 4th the party reached the mouth of the Paria and on the 5th they entered the Marble Gorge. They strained and sweated through two hard portages—presumably Badger and Soap Creek rapids—and had to repair one boat whose bottom was stove in on a rock. "The next morning," writes William Culp Darrah in *Powell of the Colorado*, "the men and boats were ready to get under way and head into the rapids—one per mile. The men were suffering more each day from exposure and hunger. The constant wetting, perspiring, and insufficient food, were beginning to tell on everyone, but least

of all on the Major. Actually, his infirmity, which prevented him from doing some of the difficult physical labor, preserved his resistance. Each portage exhausted the men a little more and sapped morale as well as strength."

The Little Colorado river was reached on August 10th —"a loathsome little stream," Sumner states in his diary, "as disgusting as there is on the continent; 3 rods wide and about 3 feet deep, half of its volume and 2/3 of its weight is mud and salt." Despite the Major's assertion at this point that "the men talk as cheerfully as ever," the fact was that they were grumbling. "If Major does not do something soon I fear the consequences," Bradley says in his journal, "but he is contented and seems to think that biscuit made of sour and musty flour and a few dried apples is ample to sustain a laboring man. If he can only study geology he will be happy without food or shelter, but the rest of us are not afflicted with it to an alarming extent." They resumed their descent on the 13th, and on the next day the Major notes: "At daybreak we walk down the bank of the river, on a little sandy beach, to take a view of a new feature in the canyon. Heretofore, hard rocks have given us bad river; soft rocks, smooth water; and a series of rocks harder than any we have experienced sets in. The river enters the granite! We can see but a little way into the granite gorge, but it looks threatening."

The men soon came to rapids imprisoned in such sheer walls that lining or portaging was thought impossible. They had no choice but to run the rapids, and run them they did. "And now we go on through this solemn, mysterious way. The river is very deep, the canyon very narrow, and still obstructed, so that there is no steady flow of the stream; but the waters wheel, and roll, and boil, and we are scarcely able to determine where we can go. Now, the boat is carried to the right, perhaps close to the wall; again, she is shot into the stream, and perhaps is dragged over to the other side, where, caught in a whirlpool, she spins about. We can neither land nor run as we please. The boats are entirely unmanageable; no order in their running can be preserved; now one, now another, is ahead, each crew laboring for its own preservation."

The weather, alternately torrid and cold and wet, added to their misery, but the men's spirits picked up a bit on the 21st, when the sombre granite of the Inner Gorge walls gave way to friendlier limestone. They made some good runs in the next few days, thirty-five miles on the 25th and another thirty-five on the 26th. But on the 27th they ran once again into the "dreaded granite," and at noon came upon what Bradley described as "the worst rapid yet seen." That did it for three of the men. The afternoon was spent scrambling over the cliffs on both sides of the river and studying the rapid to find a way through, and the Major decided there was a practicable course. But after dinner O. G. Howland asked Powell to have a talk with him, and together they walked off a short distance, out of hearing of the others. To go on, Howland claimed, would be suicidal, and he urged the Major to halt the expedition here. In any case, he, his brother Seneca, and Bill Dunn would go no farther on the river, and would rather take their chance on climbing out and reaching the Mormon towns to the north, an unknown distance across an unmapped desert. The Major argued and pleaded but Howland would not be swayed. After the men had fallen asleep Powell paced up and down on the sand, considering the situation. With his sextant he shot the stars, and calculated that he was only forty-five air line miles from the mouth of the Virgin River, which was known territory. He awakened Howland and told him this, but Howland merely shrugged and went back to sleep.

Breakfast the next morning was "as solemn as a funeral." The elder Howland and Dunn, thoroughly distrustful by then of Powell's leadership, were still determined to leave the party; Seneca Howland tried to talk them into staying, but, failing in this, elected to go with his brother. The three men were ferried across the river, given guns, ammunition, and some biscuits, and departed northward up Separation Canyon, as the tributary was henceforth to be called. Powell and his remaining crew of five decided to leave the weakest of the boats, and cached the barometers, pottery, minerals, and fossils —all their meager scientific collection—in the hope of picking them up some later year. Then they once more took to the boats. They plunged into the rapid which had moved the Howlands and Dunn to quit—and both boats sailed through it right side up. Six and a half miles farther down they came to another stretch of very bad water, and ran it safely. This was their last trial. On the 29th of August they passed the Grand Wash Cliffs and saw spread out before them a rolling desert of black bush and creosote bush. The "Great Unknown" had been explored. The continent's last unmapped wilderness had been traversed and roughly measured and charted.

"Now the danger is over," Powell writes, "now the toil has ceased; now the gloom has disappeared; now the firmament is bounded only by the horizon; and what a vast expanse of constellations can be seen.

"The river rolls by us in silent majesty; the quiet of the camp is sweet; our joy is almost ecstasy. We sit till long after midnight, talking of the Grand Canyon, talking of home, but chiefly talking of the three men who left us. Are they wandering in those depths, unable to find a way out? Are they searching over the desert lands above for water, or are they nearing the settlements?"

The three men, as Powell learned later, were dead. They had somehow climbed out of the Canyon and reached the plateau above, only to be ambushed and killed, allegedly by Shivwits Indians who, the story goes, mistook them for marauding miners.

Powell emerged from the Grand Canyon a national hero—and had the rather macabre fun of reading the glowing obituaries that the newspapers had prematurely printed about him. He succeeded in interesting Congress in a second Colorado River Expedition, obtained a ten thousand dollar appropriation in 1870, and a further grant in the session of 1871–1872 for a topographical and geological survey of the Colorado and Green rivers. And on May 22, 1871, Major Powell embarked once again at Green River, Wyoming—seated in an armchair strapped to the deck of his boat. The seven men in his party included young Dellenbaugh, who sketched and mapped his way down the river, and A. H. Thompson, Powell's brother-in-law and a geographer whose work on the trip contributed much to its success. Powell made little mention of the second trip in his reports—his *Exploration of the Colorado River*, published in 1875, intercalates several happenings of the second descent in what is purportedly an account of the first—and lamentably he never gave credit to the men who accompanied and helped him in 1871–1872.

The second expedition's purpose was to verify and to extend the scientific investigations of the first, which had been limited by the difficulties of the voyage and the loss of instruments and equipment en route. Also, the first photographs of the Colorado canyons were to be taken, and the party included photographer E. O. Beaman with his cumbersome wet-plate equipment. For five months Powell and his men cruised down the Green and the Colorado, surveying, exploring, mapping and photographing as they went. Then in November they went into winter camp, with a base camp at Houserock Springs whence they moved to the Kanab area. The next ten months were spent exploring the high plateaus rimming the Grand Canyon, and Professor Thompson directed a triangulation grid from which the first detailed map of the Colorado river country was drawn. In August 1872 the men assembled once more at Lee's Lonely Dell for the trip downriver. They proceeded, with their full share of adventures, through Grand Canyon as far as the mouth of Kanab Creek, where on September 10, 1872, Powell suddenly announced to the men that the voyage was over. The decision took the men by surprise—they had expected to continue on down to the Virgin. Perhaps, it has been suggested, Powell had not the heart to retrace the course of the last part of his first journey and revisit Separation Canyon, where the Howlands and Dunn had walked out to their death.

Powell was far more than an explorer; he was more than a man of science interested in details of topography or geology. He was a man of vision, who developed his observations into a far-sighted "general plan" for the arid lands of the West. This plan, writes Wallace Stegner, "involved whole new concepts of law, new patterns of economic and political and social organization, new designs for agriculture, whole philosophies of co-operation and government assistance. What he proposed was rendered absolutely essential by the nature of western terrain and western climate . . . But what he proposed was totally at odds with the myths and shibboleths of the main western settlement, with the fantasies of the common man and the 160-acre farm, the yeoman freehold that had supposedly bred and perpetuated the self-reliance of better-watered frontiers."

The United States Geological Survey, which he directed from 1881 to 1894, was a first implementation of Powell's "plan." So, at least in its early concept, was the Bureau of Reclamation, created in 1902. "Listened to in time," Stegner says, "[Powell] might have spared us many things: the dust bowls of the 1930's, the dust bowls of Texas in the 1950's; the acrimonious and snarled lawsuits among states for the water of the great interstate rivers; the erosion and loss of soil, the ruin of watersheds, the floods that in the lower reaches of the great rivers bear testimony to the malpractices on the headwaters. At the end of the 1880's he almost had it in his grasp, and then the politicians and the western land and cattle and water interests broke him. He retired to spend his last years in the conduct of his Bureau of Ethnology [of the Smithsonian Institution], which had systematized and remade the study of the American Indian, and in the writing of philosophical treatises that no one understood."

It should be emphasized before passing on that though he was a man of vision, Powell was no visionary. He had a firm concept of the possible and the practical. In 1893 he attended the First International Irrigation Congress, gathered in Los Angeles with several hundred delegates from more than twenty states and territories and a dozen foreign countries. One of the slogans was "a million forty acre farms" to be developed by irrigation of lands in the public domain. Powell was so appalled by the unrealistic propaganda that he scrapped his prepared speech. Rising to the rostrum he shocked and infuriated many of the delegates with an extemporaneous address that began:

"I have decided on the spur of the moment not to present the paper I have prepared, instead I shall tell you a few facts about the arid region.

"I wish to make clear to you, there is not enough water to irrigate all the lands; there is not sufficient water to irrigate all the lands which could be irrigated, only a small portion can be irrigated. It is not right to speak about the area of the public domain in terms of acres that extend over the land but in terms of acres that can be supplied with water. Gentlemen it may be unpleasant for me to give you these facts. I hesitated a good deal but finally concluded to do so. I tell you gentlemen, you are piling up a heritage of conflict and litigation of water rights, for there is not sufficient water to supply the land."

Not sufficient water to supply the land. This Colorado River, apparently so mighty as it surged by our Soap Creek camp with the tumult and din of a stormy sea, was from a wider point of view a mere trickle in the desert. Yet the visionaries of the Southwest—the land speculators, the developers, the chambers of commerce, the politicians—would count on its insufficient and undependable flow to accomplish what only the ocean or a change of climate could do: to permit accelerated expansion of the population and the economy of a desert land already developed far beyond its water supply. And the Bureau of Reclamation, intent on its own Parkinsonian empire-building, would play along.

With these thoughts we left the driftwood fire and scattered over the beach to our individual sleeping bags. Soon we were asleep, lulled into unconsciousness by the music of the rapid. Some time later the light awakened me, and I thought wearily for a moment that it was already dawn. But I opened my eyes just in time to see the full moon appear over the black canyon wall across the river. Its light bathed our beach, and every rock, every sleeping figure was boldly outlined against the light sand. I went back to sleep, and woke up again a few hours later. The view was like the negative of the picture at moonrise. The sky was now dark, our beach was in shadow. But the opposite wall of the gorge was brilliantly illuminated. The light seemed to emanate from its cliffs and terraces, as if the rocks had possessed a phosphorescence of their own.

PHILIP HYDE: *Boulder detail, near 25 Mile Rapid*

Flowers changed the face of the planet. Without them, the world we know—
even man himself—would never have existed. Francis Thompson, the English
poet, once wrote that one could not pluck a flower without troubling a star.
Intuitively he had sensed like a naturalist the enormous interlinked complexity
of life.

LOREN EISELEY

4. Marble Gorge

THE AIR was brisk as we took off the next morning, and a bank of cirrus clouds was moving in from the west foreboding a change of weather. The river had come up two or three feet during the night, and was colored coffee brown by its load of silt. It seemed swifter, too, than the first day, and in a matter of minutes we had reached our first objective, the mouth of Salt Water Wash. After bouncing through a riffle, we pulled upstream a short distance on an eddy and landed on the east shore. While Pat Reilly scrambled around the streamside ledges searching for an old inscription, we looked about us botanizing and scrutinizing the sand and rocks for signs of animal life. Primroses were in bloom; some grasses, yuccas and a few cacti, typical desert species, had found root in the dry wash; also the green branching stems of ephedra, that peculiar leafless plant from which a drink is brewed, hence its popular names, Indian tea, squaw tea or Mormon tea. A kingfisher clattered by, heading up the main canyon. A ringtailed cat—not a cat at all, but a pretty cousin of the raccoon with large eyes and a long banded tail—had left clear prints in the sand. Some house finches flitted about; a bright orange female collared lizard skittered across the rocks. A ten-inch chuckwalla scrambled up to a rock promontory and halted there, looking down at us with unblinking eyes. Soon we found another, a young one as we could tell by the black and yellow bands on its tail. It retreated into a rock crevice as we approached and lay there motionless. If we had tried to pull it out we would have failed: it would instantly have sucked in air and bloated itself till it jammed tight. Inhospitable as it might look to some human eyes, this lonely side-canyon was home to a microcosm of living things.

"Here is it, I've found it," Pat Reilly's voice suddenly called out. I walked over to him and saw the inscription, pecked into the face of a ledge a dozen feet above the river. It read:

F. M. Brown   Pres. D.C.C. & P.R.R. Co.

was drowned July 10, 1889 opposite this point

No Colorado River voyage except Major Powell's ever had a more ambitious purpose than the Brown-Stanton expedition of 1889. None had less luck at first. On May 25, 1889, Frank M. Brown, president of the Denver, Colorado Canyon, and Pacific Railroad Company, and Robert Brewster Stanton, chief engineer of the expedition, embarked at Green River Station, Utah, with the purpose of surveying a "water-level" railroad route along the Colorado to the coast. They were outfitted with five keel-bottomed hunting and pleasure boats and an ordinary flat-hulled skiff; they had provisions for only seventy-five days; and they carried no life preservers. Disaster went along for the ride. Most of the provisions were lost in a rapid in upper Cataract Canyon; the cook boat was dashed to pieces on a rock, with the loss of all cooking utensils. Battered and exhausted, their remaining boats badly damaged, the party reached Lee's Ferry—and there they should have quit. Instead they picked up some supplies and continued down into Marble Gorge on July 9. The next day Brown's boat capsized at Mile 12.0 (river mileages are all computed from Lee's Ferry.) Brown was quickly sucked under, and was never seen again. After waiting there all day hoping that the river would deliver his body, the party, now led by Stanton, moved on—but not until Peter Hansbrough had chipped the memorial inscription into the rock. Five days later, below Twenty-five Mile Rapid, Hansbrough was drowned along with Henry Richards. (Like the ill-fated Esteban, Richards too was a Negro.)

Stanton decided that this was tragedy enough for one trip, and at Mile 32.0 gave the order to abandon the river. But it was only a strategic retreat. Five months later Stanton was back on the river with a party of twelve. This time they started below Cataract Canyon with three sturdy, specially built boats—and life preservers for all hands. The photographer, F. A. Nims, broke a leg in a fall in Marble Gorge and Stanton and his men performed a miracle in carrying him out over a 1,700-foot wall to a point on the plateau which could be reached by wagon. Another man left the expedition at Crystal Canyon; three more, having proved useless in work details, were ordered out at Diamond Creek, but on April 26, 1890, Stanton and his remaining crew reached tidewater on the Gulf of California in Mexico.

Along the way over two thousand photographs were taken, and amazingly not a single negative was lost on the trip. A continuous transit line was run for the first

This song of the waters is audible to every ear, but there is other music in these hills, by no means audible to all. . . . On a still night, when the campfire is low and the Pleiades have climbed over rimrocks, sit quietly and listen . . . and think hard of everything you have seen and tried to understand. Then you may hear it—a vast pulsing harmony—its score inscribed on a thousand hills, its notes the lives and deaths of plants and animals, its rhythms spanning the seconds and the centuries. ALDO LEOPOLD

355 miles, levels were taken and contour topography sketched. Below Glen Canyon, time permitted only a more superficial survey except where greater declivities, sharper curves or other factors made more detail necessary. Even so, Stanton was satisfied that the Grand Canyon line was "neither impossible nor impracticable" and that the costs of construction and maintenance would be "reasonable" especially when compared with other transcontinental railways, which must cross high mountain passes.

As for possible traffic and profits, Stanton thought the outlook most promising. The principal freight would be coal from the Colorado mines, which he estimated could be delivered in San Diego at from a half to a third of the going market price. Additional freight would be won by the lure of a year-round route through the high country, unaffected by winter storms, and the line would benefit by facilitating the settlement and exploitation of the natural resources of the area through which it would run. Finally, Stanton expected that the thrill of a train trip through the superb gorges of the Colorado River would prove irresistible to transcontinental travelers.

Only three decades had passed since Ives' prediction that "this profitless locality" would be "forever unvisited and undisturbed," and here was Stanton, urging the profitability of building a railroad that would take thousands of passengers a year through the depths of the Grand Canyon. But plausible as his arguments might have been, the financial backers of the D.C.C. & P.R.R. Company remained unconvinced, and the ambitious survey which had cost three lives was pigeonholed.

As we boarded the boats again and pushed off into the current, I was grateful that Stanton's advice had gone unheeded; that no railbed scarred the cliff bench to our left, no trestles or bridges intruded on the mystery of the side canyons; that the rumble of a freight train, the whistle of a locomotive did not pierce the lonely silence of the Marble Gorge; that its majesty was as yet unimpaired by being made to serve men's wants.

To those who take it as dogma that nothing is of value until put to use by man, my feeling would seem absurd—if not hypocritical and selfish. Were we not making use of the Marble Gorge to satisfy our peculiar idea of pleasure—running rapids in little wooden boats? Did we, and other river runners, not oppose its being dammed just so that we might continue to enjoy our sport—at the cost of the greater good of the far greater number?

No.

It was possible that none of us who took part on this trip would ever traverse the Grand Canyon again. But that did not matter. What did matter was that the possibility of enjoying this unique experience must not be foreclosed to all men for all time. What mattered also was that the Grand Canyon was one of the marvels of the world where nature's work had achieved such splendor that it would be sacrilegious to alter it in any way. The wildness of the Canyon, and the possibility of immersing oneself in that wildness which the river affords, must be preserved in a world where wildness is everywhere in retreat before creeping civilization. Descending the Colorado through the Grand Canyon is one of those undertakings, like climbing Mount Everest, that appeal to the romantic imagination of man. Except that, unlike Everest, the Colorado demands no unusual physical gifts, and more and more people have discovered while descending it the uplift of the soul which can come from two or three weeks' intimacy with one of nature's grandest works. Take away the *possibility* of having this experience, and even those who might never themselves seek the elation of running the Colorado's rapids will have been swindled of a birthright—for the world will be that much duller for everyone.

Wallace Stegner once wrote of Utah's Robber's Roost country, not far to the north of Grand Canyon: "It is a lovely and terrible wilderness, such a wilderness as Christ and the prophets went out into; harshly and beautifully colored, broken and worn until its bones are exposed, its great sky without a smudge of taint from Technocracy, and in hidden corners and pockets under its cliffs the sudden poetry of springs. Save a piece of country like that intact, and it does not matter in the slightest that only a few people every year will go into it. That is precisely its value. Roads would be a desecration, crowds would ruin it. But those who haven't the strength or youth to go into it and live with it can still drive up onto the shoulder of the Aquarius Plateau and simply sit and look . . . And if they can't even get to the places on the Aquarius where present roads will carry them, they can simply contemplate the *idea*, take pleasure in the fact that such a timeless and uncontrolled part of earth is still there.

"These are some of the things wilderness can do for us. That is the reason we need to put into effect, for its preservation, some other principle than the principles of exploitation or usefulness or even recreation. We simply need that wild country available to us, even if we never do more than drive to its edge and look in. For it can be a means of reassuring ourselves of our sanity as creatures, a part of the geography of hope."

. . . And now, the scenery is on a grand scale. The walls of the canyon, 2500 feet high, are of marble, of many beautiful colors, and often polished below by the waves, or far up the sides, where showers have washed the sands over the cliffs. At one place I have a walk, for more than a mile, on a marble pavement, all polished and fretted with strange devices, and embossed in a thousand fantastic patterns. Through a cleft in the wall the sun shines on this pavement, which gleams in iridescent beauty.

JOHN WESLEY POWELL

P. T. REILLY: Royal Arches, Mile 41.5

Substitute "Grand Canyon" or "Marble Gorge" for Aquarius Plateau, and Stegner's words would remain as true. The Marble Gorge, too, is a part of this geography of hope. The farther we penetrated it, the more magnificent it became. The river seemed to have a giddy slope, and rapid followed rapid in quick succession: Sheer-wall, Hot Na Na, Houserock, North Canyon, Twenty-one, Twenty-two, Twenty-three, Twenty-four, and Twenty-four-and-a-half Mile rapids. The uptilt of the strata in the Canyon's walls increased the illusion of plunging into the earth. The Supai formation, with alternate beds of sandstone and shale, had appeared along the shore soon after our departure from Soap Creek, and where the river cut through its harder members, red cliffs, often beautifully cross-bedded, shot straight up from the water's edge. The Canyon narrowed as it grew deeper, and as dark rainclouds closed in overhead we felt more and more boxed in, tiny and unimportant—of no greater consequence in the order of things than those blue-winged teal flying by or those otters who had left their tracks on the beach.

We camped at the head of Twenty-five Mile Rapid, where Hansbrough and Richards had met their deaths, and had the booming of its waves as a lullaby. The storm that had threatened all afternoon finally broke during the night, and rain kept trickling in under my poncho and wetting my sleeping bag. I tried several times to rearrange the poncho, without much success, and finally stopped worrying about the rain, deciding it was better to sleep wet than not to sleep at all. And except for the evidence of my damp bedroll the next morning the night's rain might have been a dream, for we awoke at dawn to the sight of a clear sky, with only scattered wisps of cloud overhead. We got under way just as the sun peeped over the east rim, and all three boats boomed through Twenty-five Mile Rapid scarcely shipping a drop.

Now we were entering the most beautiful part of the Marble Gorge. The Redwall limestone had appeared and formed the lower stratum of the Canyon walls. Throughout the Grand Canyon, this limestone constitutes what is perhaps the most striking single feature, a sheer red cliff five hundred feet high or more. Here too, the Redwall presented a characteristic verticality, which became more and more impressive as each mile we traveled added another fifty feet or so to its height. The overlying layers were set back in a series of tiers and slopes, and this setback kept them generally from being visible from the river, except at either end of the straight sections of the gorge where the upper cliffs curved above the Redwall as the Colorado rounded a bend. At times we got a glimpse of the upper walls through narrow slots cut into the Redwall by tributary creeks: it was like peeking through a keyhole. In these slots the limestone was worn smooth and almost shiny, and its natural gray-blue color showed through—the Redwall is red only because stained by iron oxides washed down from the red Hermit and Supai formations above. These waterfall notches were dry in this season, but I could imagine the beauty they would add to the scene when gushing after a summer thunderstorm.

Shafts of sun poured through the notches on the east wall of the gorge, and shone on the dark water of the river. The contrasts of shadowed and brightly lit water delighted our photographers, who never tired of catching a boat silhouetted by the slanting sunbeams against the darker background of the gorge. The details of the Redwall were endlessly fascinating to photographer and non-photographer alike: magnificent fluting along the river banks, niches and recesses and alcoves above, innumerable small and large caves—the openings of anastomotic tubes, solution channels which followed the eastward tilt of the bedding plane of the rock and which were likely to cause a major loss of water if the Marble Gorge Dam were built.

Toward noon we reached a point where the Redwall became even more fantastic. It was horizontally banded with light and dark stripes, and the scene might have been out of a child's fairytale book, with rocks made of peppermint candy. This aspect of the Canyon had suggested to Powell the name "Marble Gorge"—although marble is actually *metamorphosed* limestone and there is no such rock in the Marble Gorge. Between these candy-striped walls we drifted on down, and came to a point where a beautiful stair-step canyon entered from the right. Just below it we landed at Vasey's Paradise, named by Powell for a botanist friend. Out of the Redwall, a third of the way up its face, gushed two strong jets of clear water. The streams fell straight for a small distance, then were broken by the banding of the rock into a sequence of short falls, as water might run down garden steps during a heavy rain. Alongside the falls and below them plants grew in lush profusion, an oasis of fresh greenery that contrasted agreeably with the otherwise arid aspect of the Canyon walls. Redbud was past its peak, but enough were still in bloom to waft a delicate fragrance into the air. A cascade of scarlet monkeyflowers tumbled down the slope; the whorled stems of horsetails grew thickly among the rocks; and everywhere the shiny leaves of poison ivy glistened in the sun. How poison ivy had found this place puzzled me—I had never seen

P. T. REILLY: Sunset near Nankoweap Creek, Mile 52.8

The cliffs below Vasey's Paradise are unrivalled in the whole Grand Canyon series save possibly by those in the vicinity of the mouth of Havasu Creek. . . . Quiet smooth-flowing water gave us opportunity to revel in the veritable symphony of colors undisturbed by navigational worries.

LEWIS R. FREEMAN

any in my months at the Grand Canyon, nor were we to find it elsewhere along the river. But it was another instance of nature providing a niche for a species, and somehow seeing to it that the species found the niche.

The water from these springs was cold and delicious, and we refilled all our containers before moving on. The river here bent sharply to the east, and for a little over a mile we rowed along on quiet water, basking in the warmth of the afternoon sun trapped between the lofty sides of the gorge. Just how lofty they were we came to realize as we approached the next bend where the river again curved southwest. At the foot of the left wall there appeared a low cave, the height of its mouth about a third of the width. We had been noticing caves all day, and if this one in particular caught our attention it was at first only because of its situation right at the water's edge and the graceful shape of the entrance arch. But as we approached, the *Susie Too* ahead of us seemed to shrink before our eyes. The mouth of the cave yawned wider and wider and higher and higher until, landing at the great sweep of beach beneath it, we took measure of its real immensity. This was Redwall Cavern, described by Powell as a "vast semi-circular chamber which, if utilized for a theater, would give sitting room to fifty thousand people." He was exaggerating, but not by very much. A hundred yards wide, fifty deep and thirty high was my guess as we walked into its cool shade. The sand of its floor was criss-crossed with lizard, mouse and insect tracks, and we looked for signs of bats but found none. Viewed from inside the cavern the world outside looked like a painting by an abstractionist with a penchant for curved surfaces of contrasting colors: the swell of the white sand dunes at its mouth, the long brown curve of the river, the round crimson bastion of the Redwall across the water, the arc of blue sky framed between the opposite cliff and the vault of the cave. Everything in this setting was bold—the clashing colors, the intense sunlight, the heroic proportions.

We moved on after an hour and soon began to look for a possible campsite. Sandy beaches were frequent, pleasant spots fringed with willow and tamarisk that offered all the "amenities" for a comfortable camp except the essential driftwood. Devonian Alcove was particularly alluring with the odor of redbud permeating the air, but it, too, had no wood. We entered a nearly straight north-south aisle of the Canyon and there, ahead of us, was the proposed site for the dam. A wooden raft was anchored off the left shore. On both sides of the gorge, twin steel scaffolds climbed perhaps two hundred feet up the Redwall. Test tunnels had been drilled and blasted into the sides of the gorge, and tailings from these tunnels partially obliterated the beach on our left. Still there was ample room to camp, and what was more there was wood, so we hove to for the night. After dinner we threw branches from a dead catclaw onto our fire. They burned with hot, crackling flames which cast a faint red glow onto the Canyon wall across the river from us. To Joe Hall, sleeping here felt like "camping in the bottom of an immense shoe box." As for me, I pictured myself as a fish in a tank. I imagined the weight of three hundred feet of water above my head—the three hundred feet of water which would fill this gorge if the dam were built and the river filled the reservoir behind it. I saw Redwall Cavern submerged, Vasey's Paradise lost, the candy-striped walls obliterated, the graceful beaches buried, the native plants and animals evicted or drowned, the living river, with its varied moods of fury and tranquility, replaced by the monotony of a reservoir lake. Even Stanton's railroad line might have been preferable to that.

. . . At a bend where the river turned sharply to the east a wall glittered as if set with gems, and on coming nearer they found springs bursting from the cliffs high up and sheeting the rock in rainbows. Below was a garden of incredible green, moss and maidenhair and redbud and hackberry and ferns. They named it Vasey's Paradise, after their last year's botanist from Bloomington.

As they went on the walls grew higher, and still higher, and great buttresses thrust out into the channel to block the river into coves and twist it in whirlpools. But here the channel was wider, the river less swift, so that they could take a more leisurely look at the marble chambers and alcoves and caves. Through the gates of flaring canyons that came in from the right, draining the lofty table of the Kaibab westward, they saw the piney back of that noble plateau.

WALLACE STEGNER

PHILIP HYDE: *Vasey's Paradise, Mile 31.9*

The Living Shore

. . . Everything is superlative, transcending the power of the intelligence to comprehend it. There is no central point or object around which the other elements are grouped and to which they are tributary. The grandest objects are merged in a congregation of others equally grand. Hundreds of these mighty structures, miles in length, and thousands of feet in height, rear their majestic heads out of the abyss, displaying their richly-molded plinths and friezes, thrusting out their gables, wing-walls, buttresses, and pilasters, and recessed with alcoves and panels. If any one of these stupendous creations had been planted upon the plains of central Europe it would have influenced modern art as profoundly as Fujiyama has influenced the decorative art of Japan. Yet here they are all swallowed up in the confusion of multitude.

CLARENCE E. DUTTON

If there is magic on this planet, it is contained in water. . . .

Once in a lifetime, perhaps, one escapes the actual confines of the flesh. Once in a lifetime, if one is lucky, one so merges with sunlight and air and running water that whole eons, the eons that mountains and deserts know, might pass in a single afternoon without discomfort. The mind has sunk away into its beginnings among old roots and the obscure tricklings and movings that stir inanimate things. Like the charmed fairy circle into which a man once stepped, and upon emergence learned that a whole century had passed in a single night, one can never quite define this secret; but it has something to do, I am sure, with common water. Its substance reaches everywhere; it touches the past and prepares the future; it moves under the poles and wanders thinly in the heights of air. It can assume forms of exquisite perfection in a snowflake, or strip the living to a single shining bone cast up by the sea.

LOREN EISELEY

PHILIP HYDE: River near mouth of Tapeats Creek, Mile 133.7

...Across Hutton's pages pass a series of small natural operations that over long time periods erode mountains, create valleys, and that, if mountain-building processes did not counteract their effect, would bring whole continents down to sea level.

He saw the bit of soil carried away by a mountain brook or a spring freshet lodge in and nourish a lower valley; he saw the wind endlessly polishing and eroding stones on the high flanks of the world. He saw, with the marvelous all-seeing eye of Shakespeare, that "water-drops have worn the stones of Troy and blind oblivion swallowed cities up." He knew about the constant passage of water from sea to land and back again. If a leaf fell he knew where it was bound, and multiplied it mentally by ten thousand leaves in ten thousand, thousand autumns. One has the feeling that he sensed, on his remote Scottish farm, when frost split a stone on a winter night. Or when one boulder, poised precariously on a far mountain side, fell after a thousand years. For him and him alone, the water dripping from the cottagers' eaves had become Niagaras falling through unplumbed millennia. "Nature," he wrote simply, "lives in motion." Every particle in the world was hurrying somewhere, or was so destined in the long traverse of time.

LOREN EISELEY

PHILIP HYDE: Boulder mosaic, Nankoweap Creek, Mile 52.3

It is a peculiar feature of these walls that many projections are set out into the river, as if the wall was buttressed for support. The walls themselves are half a mile high, and these buttresses are on a corresponding scale, jutting into the river scores of feet. In the recesses between these projections there are quiet bays, except at the foot of a rapid, when there are dancing eddies or whirlpools. Sometimes these alcoves have caves at the back, giving them the appearance of great depth. Then other caves are seen above, forming vast dome-shaped chambers. The walls and buttresses and chambers are all of marble.

JOHN WESLEY POWELL

But our civilization is rapidly becoming one in which only two values are recognized: power and amusement. It would be a pity if the last refuges where man can enter into another kind of relation with the natural world should be improved out of existence by even the most well meaning. The park system of which Grand Canyon is so striking a part was planned by men who spoke of "preserving" certain of the grandest examples of the American continent's natural beauties. Gradually one has heard less and less about "preserving," more and more about "development" and "utilization for recreation." The two ideals are neither identical nor even compatible.

JOSEPH WOOD KRUTCH

PHILIP HYDE: Dune and pool, mouth of Comanche Creek, Mile 67.5

The canyon would be essentially 'dead' if the living river were stilled . . . We will convert the canyon from a working geological laboratory into a museum piece, a petrified instant-in-time. But I question whether this is truly the full extent of the damage we stand to do. What happens to the form of a canyon when the river which carved it stops flowing?

We would have taken the authority on ourselves to reverse the direction of the canyon's development. Such an action would foreclose forever the chance that the distant future would see an even more spectacular canyon than we know today. Are we to assume—a classic mistake—that the superlatives of our own experience constitute ultimate expressions?

Larry R. Harrington

The Parks are set aside for other than dollar uses, to be kept without impairment for the enjoyment of the people. They cannot tolerate exploitation of any resource, for exploitation uses up, makes over, mars, and changes the things that according to wise law must be kept natural. If a tree falls in a Park, unless it blocks a road or endangers a building or human life it must lie where it has fallen, slowly to return to the earth out of which it grew. Grass can renew itself if properly used and cared for; so can a forest. But a mountain or a canyon or archæological remains cannot. If you cut a great swath up a hillside to put in a ski lift, the gash will remain for a very long time, perhaps long after you have abandoned the lift. If you flood a canyon, . . . that canyon is gone forever, buried first under water and eventually under silt. And the lake you create will not be there for many generations to see or use. It has been stated on good authority that 38 per cent of our dams have a useful life of under fifty years. . . .

Moreover, no permanent growth can take hold on the shores of a reservoir if the water fluctuates as much as ten feet. The margin of any draw-down reservoir is a broad ugly mudbank except at extreme high water—and the average reservoir is full no oftener than once in four years. When I saw it in October 1954, the lake behind Fontana Dam in the Great Smokies was something dismal to behold. After three dry summers the water had receded many, many yards, exposing bleak banks of dried mud, bare of vegetation of any sort. There is no pleasure is sailing on such a lake as that, no pleasure in swimming in it, certainly none in looking at it . . .

Alfred A. Knopf

PHILIP HYDE: *Evening Primrose at Granite Falls Rapid, Mile 93.5*

. . . I find most interesting the conspiracy of life in the desert to circumvent the death rays of the all-conquering sun. The beaten earth appears defeated and dead, but it only appears so. A vast and inventive organization of living matter survives by seeming to have lost. The gray and dusty sage wears oily armor to protect its inward small moistness. Some plants engorge themselves with water in the rare rainfall and store it for future use. Animal life wears a hard, dry skin or an outer skeleton to defy the desiccation. And every living thing has developed techniques for finding or creating shade. . . .

JOHN STEINBECK

PHILIP HYDE: *Near water's edge, 25 Mile Rapid*

Yet people are beginning to suspect that the greatest freedom is not achieved by sheer irresponsibility. The earth is common ground and we are its overlords, whether we hold title or not. Gradually the idea is taking form that the land must be held in safe keeping, that one generation is to some extent responsible to the next; and that it is contrary to the public good to allow an individual . . . to destroy almost beyond repair any part of the soil or the water or even the view!

E. B. White

For there are some people who can live without wild things about them and the earth beneath their feet, and some who cannot. To those of us who, in a city, are always aware of the abused and abased earth below the pavement, walking on grass, watching the flight of birds, or finding the first spring dandelion are rights as old and unalienable as the rights to life, liberty and the pursuit of happiness. We belong to no cult. We are not Nature Lovers. We don't love nature any more than we love breathing. Nature is simply something indispensable, like air and light and water, that we accept as necessary to living, and the nearer we can get to it the happier we are.

Louise Dickenson Rich

PHILIP HYDE: *Dune near Monument Creek, Mile 93.5*

But in lonely places the tone of the raven's comment seems to change. . . . It is a lonesome sound, so most people say. But not so lonesome as no sound other than the wind in the trees or the rattle of a stone which has waited millions of years for this particular moment when it has been ordained that the Canyon shall be widened by precisely its half-inch width. At least the raven is, like us, a creature confined to a narrower band of time and, like us, conscious of certain things whether he be conscious of time or not.

JOSEPH WOOD KRUTCH

PHILIP HYDE: *Red Canyon at Hance Rapid, Mile 76.7*

The river is now quiet; the canyon wider. Above, when the river is at its flood, the waters gorge up, so that the difference between high and low water mark is often 50 or even 70 feet, but here high-water mark is not more than 20 feet above the present stage of the river. Sometimes there is a narrow flood plain between the water and the wall. Here we first discover mesquite shrubs, —small trees with finely divided leaves and pods, somewhat like the locust.

JOHN WESLEY POWELL

... Part of our love must be expressed by our relation to all living organisms and organic structures; some of our love must go to sea and river and soil, restraining careless exploitation and pollution; the trees and wild creatures of the forest, the fish in the rivers, are as subject to our affectionate care as the dogs or the cats who live in closer dependence on us. Consider the systematic wiping out of the natural landscape and the withdrawal from rural occupations and rural ways that took place during the past century: the spread of megalopolitan deserts undercuts love at its very base because it removes man's sense of active partnership and fellowship in the common processes of growth, which bind him to other organisms. When such habits prevail, love is reduced to a thin verbal precept, not a daily practice....

LEWIS MUMFORD

HILIP HYDE: Red Canyon

But though the inherent colors are less intense than some others, yet under the quickening influence of the atmosphere they produce effects to which all others are far inferior. And here language fails and description becomes impossible. . . .. A perpetual glamor envelops the landscape. Things are not what they seem, and the perceptions cannot tell us what they are. . . .

In truth, the tone and temper of the landscape are constantly varying, and the changes in its aspect are very great. It is never the same, even from day to day, or even from hour to hour. In the early morning its mood and subjective influences are usually calmer and more full of repose than at other times, but as the sun rises higher the whole scene is so changed that we cannot recall our first impressions. Every passing cloud, every change in the position of the sun, recasts the whole. At sunset the pageant closes amid splendors that seem more than earthly. The direction of the full sunlight, the massing of the shadows, the manner in which the side lights are thrown in from the clouds determine these modulations, and the sensitiveness of the picture to the slightest variations in these conditions is very wonderful.

CLARENCE E. DUTTON

"Never have I seen such wonders or met landlords so worthy of their land. They have, and still have, the power to ravage it; and instead they have made it a garden." Thus wrote the visiting English naturalist, James Fisher, in the book called *Wild America* upon which he and Roger Tory Peterson collaborated. Nor is the tribute wholly undeserved. But Mr. Fisher politely refrained from stressing either the unearned blessing we received when we inherited the continent from a red man too little advanced technologically to have defaced it, or the fact that the "power to ravage" which the National Parks Act was intended to hold forever in check, still ominously exists.

No one opposes "conservation" as such. But many insist upon defining it in their own way. There are always rival claims to every unexploited area, and even the parks cannot stand up against such claims unless the strength of their own claim is recognized. Unless we think of intangible values as no less important than material resources, unless we are willing to say that man's need of and right to what the parks and wildernesses provide are as fundamental as any of his material needs, they are lost. . . .

JOSEPH WOOD KRUTCH

The whole country suffers every time Americans make a bad choice, even a local one, that allows the needless waste of any of our natural treasures. The destruction of such resources is irrevocable; no one can pass that way again.

LIFE EDITORIAL

NSEL ADAMS: *View down Bright Angel Canyon toward South Rim*

5. Nankoweap

STANTON'S PARTY found the body on the beach at the left of the rapid. Before it was stranded it had probably floated in the big eddy for months, circling endlessly night and day, trapped like the driftwood which also had been shunted there and would move downstream only when the river rose in the spring. They carried the body through the thicket of catclaw to the foot of the cliff, and buried him there, covering the grave with a low mound of stones. But no one would volunteer to carve the dead man's name on the rock above the grave. They were superstitious. For this had been the man who had pecked out Frank Brown's epitaph up there at Mile 12, and he had been the next to go. Finally one man, Langdon Gibson, shrugged off his superstition and chiseled the dead man's initials in the cliff: "P.M.H. 1889." Peter Hansbrough's long river journey had finally ended.

Rather subdued, we walked away from the grave and were headed back toward the boats when Joe Hall stopped us with a sign. Perched on the thorny branch of a catclaw was a minuscule mud nest, about the size and shape of a jigger glass. A female black-chinned humming-bird hovered over it, her wings a blur of motion; then she whirred over to another branch where she proceeded to groom herself, preening the feathers under each tiny wing with her needle-like beak. After a few minutes of this she darted back to the nest, and settled comfortably on it—warming with her tiny body eggs that must have been the size of peas.

We climbed back into the boats and pushed off into the eddy, plowing through a sargasso of driftwood until we were once again in the tail waves of President Harding Rapid. This rapid was rough, with a huge boulder in midchannel at its head which was nearly submerged and which we had carefully avoided. All three boats had barreled through the big waves without incident; in fact, to our surprise and delight, we had emerged from the test completely dry. But if the river had not wet us it looked as if the sky soon would. Toward noon we pulled into a beach on the right under lowering skies, and sought shelter under an overhang of the Muav limestone, which underlies the Redwall. It started to sprinkle, but the threatening shower did not materialize.

The Canyon was becoming wider and more open; its walls no longer rose straight from the river but were set back by a talus slope criss-crossed with deer trails—evidently for all its sparseness the vegetation was sufficient to support bigger things than lizards and rodents. In mid-afternoon we came to a wide, rugged canyon that entered to our right. Looking up this canyon, we could see the snowy, forested rim of the Kaibab Plateau six thousand feet above us, where dark clouds hung low over Point Imperial and Saddle Mountain. We tied up at the beach just above Nankoweap Rapid, and I took our canteens to refill them from the milky waters of the creek, which bubbled and tumbled merrily over its bed of rocks. Nankoweap Creek was only two or three feet wide, but it was obvious from the size of the canyon it had cut over the ages and from the breadth of its delta that it could be quite formidable in a flash flood. The delta was thickly grown with mesquite and catclaw, small trees of the pea family that were just coming into leaf. And the gravelly benches were a desert garden: besides the orange mallow which we had admired before and clumps of yellow flowers which I could not identify, two kinds of cacti had burst out with large brilliant blooms—the beavertails' a viscid rose, the hedgehogs' a crimson magenta.

I stopped for a close look at one of the latter when something else caught my eye. Nestled among the pebbles was a small potsherd, about two inches square. Its gray-white surface was decorated with a black chevron design, the inner V of which was further embellished with little round dots. I looked around me, and noticed there were dozens of shards strewn over the ground. Some, like the first, were white with black lines. Others had red designs on a white background, or black on red. Still others, probably from vessels of a more utilitarian nature, were unpainted but adorned with a corrugated design, as if the wet coils of clay had been pinched by the maker and marked with his or her fingernails. The "Ancient Ones"—the "Anasazi" as the Navajos call them—had lived here once. And if the potsherds were not evidence enough Pat Reilly pointed to a niche in the Redwall a little downstream from Nankoweap, in which some small buildings were nestled.

ANSEL ADAMS: *Aspen on the Kaibab Plateau*

Martin Litton, Bill Jones, and I decided to hike up to the ruins the next morning. It was a good stiff climb, about a thousand feet up a steep rocky slope and broken ledges in the lower part of the Redwall, and we were breathing a little hard as we reached our goal. Set well back under an overhang were a half dozen little rooms, each about six feet long by four high and three deep, and each having its own door to the ledge where we stood. Their construction was simple: the overhang served as a common roof, and only the front walls and the partition walls had had to be built. But they were built well, of flat rocks cemented with mud; the doors were neatly rectangular, and the front wall of each cubicle was nicely joined to that of its neighbor, together forming a curve that paralleled the back of the niche. These little structures were at the very least six centuries old, which attested not only to the skill of the builders but to the well-protected location and the dryness of the climate. Even the sticks which served as the lintels of the doorways were perfectly preserved.

I crawled into one of the rooms and stretched out on its floor, thinking that the landlord would argue that though the penthouse was a bit small the view was worth the rent. These may have just been granaries where the Indians had stored the food they probably grew along Nankoweap Creek. In one of the rooms Bill Jones found an aboriginal corn cob—exactly an inch and a quarter long—and a shard or two of corrugated ware.

Who were these ancient Canyon dwellers? Why and where had they gone? Who, if any, are their descendants today? Although over five hundred ruins have been discovered within Grand Canyon National Park—not to count those in the Canyon outside the Park—only a vague outline of the area's prehistory is known. Traces of early man have been found in the Southwest that antedate the last (or latest) Ice Age. At Tule Springs, Nevada, fire hearths dated by the carbon 14 method as 28,000 years old have produced crudely flaked tools and bone artifacts. By the end of the glaciers' retreat, some 10,000 years ago, the desert-like Great Basin to the west of the Rockies was occupied by groups of Indians who had developed a variety of special tools to use the wild foods of the region—seeds, nuts, fruits, and berries—and who hunted many animals that have become extinct in America. In Nevada, Arizona, and New Mexico, tools and weapons of these Desert Culture Indians have been found associated with the remains of mastodon, mammoth, horse, camel, giant ground sloth, tapir, musk ox, giant bison, dire wolf, and other animals which would either die out or move elsewhere on the continent.

Ground sloth bones and dung have been discovered in the Grand Canyon, at Rampart Cave and other caves near the Canyon's lower end. But the first signs of man's presence are of much more recent date. In 1957 split-twig figurines, probably representing such present-day canyon country species as deer, bighorn sheep, pronghorns and the like, were found in hard-to-reach caves in the walls of Grand Canyon. But no evidence of habitation was found in these caves; the figurines, dated by radioactive carbon methods as three thousand years old, were probably ceremonial, and the caves hunting shrines.

The first scattered remains of human occupation in the Canyon date back somewhat less than two thousand years. But by about A.D. 600 or 700, both rims of the Grand Canyon had a settled population. On the south rim lived a group whom archaeologists call Cohonina. They made primitive pottery and their houses were simple. One of these houses, occupied probably about 800 A.D., has been excavated in Grand Canyon National Park about four miles west of Desert View. The main room was a saucer-shaped depression about fifteen feet in diameter with a fire pit at its center. A rectangular framework stood inside the house, and walls had been formed by poles leaned against this frame and either plastered or covered with brush. Two small storage rooms and three storage pits adjoined the main house, and a smaller separate house was built a few feet away.

The other inhabitants of the Grand Canyon at that time were the Basketmakers. A few of them dwelt alongside the Cohonina but their main settlements were on the north rim. Archaeologists have traced these Indians' history to the early years of the Christian era, at which time they inhabited the mesa and canyon country drained by the San Juan River. A small race—the men averaged five feet four inches in height—the Basketmakers originally lived in caves or brush shelters, but by the time they settled the north rim of Grand Canyon they dwelt in pithouses, not unlike the Cohonina house. Both men and women usually went about naked, though they did make blankets woven from strips of rabbit fur wrapped around cords, and wore beautifully made sandals with cupped heel and scalloped toe. As their name implies they made baskets, of grass and yucca leaves. These were of many sizes and shapes, usually with red or black designs woven in, and many of the coiled baskets were so tightly woven that they were watertight. Corn, squash, and beans were their staples; they hunted large game with the atlatl or spearthrower; smaller game they caught in various snares and traps, many woven of women's hair, or in large nets stretched across the mouth of a canyon into which

PHILIP HYDE: *Willows and dune, near Nankoweap Creek*

hunters, working down from the head of the canyon, would drive rabbits or other game.

By 700 A.D. the Basketmakers had learned to make pottery, some of which was painted with designs like those woven into the baskets. It had also occurred to them that much labor could be saved by building two or more houses together to form a larger unit. Both innovations, pottery and multiple dwellings, made tremendous progress in the next, or Development Pueblo, period—roughly A.D. 700 to A.D. 1000. More and more houses were built together; five, ten, fifty or more rooms were constructed end to end, forming a crescent or L-shaped structure open to the southwest. Each such structure constituted a village, or, to use the Spanish word, a Pueblo. Masonry began to be used, and with it the construction of multistoried buildings became possible. At the same time the old circular, subterranean pithouse was retained, but for a specialized use. Built in the open area before the communal houses, the pithouse became the *kiva*, or ceremonial room, which Pueblo Indians still build and use.

In the Grand Canyon region the great center of Pueblo development was around Kayenta, a present-day Navajo trading center in northeastern Arizona, and the culture is referred to as the Kayenta. By the year 800, Kayenta people were building small houses along the north rim of Grand Canyon. A hundred years later the Pueblos were well established on the south rim also, having displaced the Cohonina as far as the present Hermit's Rest west of Grand Canyon Village. Crops were grown on terraces built along the drainage slopes and in the ravines; diversion dams and ditches held and channeled rainwater; produce was stored in small granaries built in cliff ledges. Cotton had been introduced, along with techniques of spinning and loom weaving, and men and women were clothed in kilts and aprons. Pottery included corrugated ware and painted ware with increasingly elaborate designs in black on white, black on red, or red on orange.

The three centuries following the year 1000 were the Classic Period of Pueblo culture. The great pueblos and cliff houses of Pueblo Bonito and Chettro Ketl in New Mexico, Mesa Verde in southwestern Colorado, and Keet Seel and Betatakin in the Kayenta area of northeast Arizona, all date from that era. Magnificent pottery, beautifully woven textiles, and fine jewelry were produced. Trade was carried on with far distant places for luxuries demanded by a society no longer wholly occupied with scratching the ground for a living: shells from the Pacific and the Gulf of California, copper bells, parrots, and macaws from Mexico. Even in their wrath the gods proved kind. At about the time William of Normandy invaded England in 1066, Indians living near the San Francisco mountains fifty miles south of the Grand Canyon witnessed the explosive birth of a new volcano. Within months Sunset Crater grew to a height of a thousand feet, burying a thousand square miles under black volcanic sand. A few Indians lost their homes in the calamity; some may have lost their lives. But before long it was noticed that the ash formed a mulch which preserved the moisture of the soil and permitted the growing of crops where none could be raised before. Soon a complex of thriving communities had developed in the area, attracting people not only from the Kayenta region but from the Hohokam to the south and Mogollón to the east as well, and bequeathing to us such impressive ruins as the Citadel and Wupatki—the latter boasting an unusual oval amphitheater and a Hohokam ball court.

But the Classic Pueblo Period left few vestiges at the Grand Canyon. The Canyon was just too rugged to support such concentrations of people as lived in the larger pueblos to the northeast and south. In fact the Classic Period still had a century to go when the north rim was abandoned in 1175. On the south rim small pueblos, containing up to 30 rooms, survived a while longer. One, Tusayán Ruin (named after the old Spanish term for the Hopi country) has been excavated near the Cohonina house. It is a U-shaped structure of limestone boulders set in clay mortar, with seven rooms in its two-story living section, two circular kivas, and two wings of small, one-story storage rooms. Perhaps 25 or 30 people lived in this pueblo, which was built between 1185 and 1200. But by 1250 Tusayán Pueblo, and all other villages in the area, were deserted, the people probably moving north to Kayenta.

They did not remain there long. For in 1276 a great drought set in that lasted with little respite for 23 years. Perhaps spurred on by enemy raids too, the Kayenta people moved south, some into the Hopi country, some still farther to the southern White Mountains. The Sunset Crater area, stripped by the winds of its ash mulch, also was abandoned, and Wupatki, the Citadel, and other pueblos of the region became ghost towns.

Of the Indians living in the Grand Canyon region today, only the Hopi can claim descent beyond reasonable doubt from the "Ancient Ones" whose ruined pueblos, farm terraces, granaries, and potsherds are scattered about the Grand Canyon. Their mesa-top villages to the southeast of the Canyon are not greatly different from the pueblos of old; in fact one of them,

PHILIP HYDE: *Sandbar opposite Lava Canyon, Mile 65.5*

It was beautiful with the only kind of beauty that I was now beginning to recognize as authentic: the great, unadorned beauty and strength of the functional. There was nothing anywhere that was unnecessary; nothing, whether the work of man or of nature, that existed without a purpose. I was a stranger; but in spite of my strangeness the country spoke to some inner need of which I had not until then been fully aware, to a need to know who I was and what I was worth. . . .

LOUISE DICKINSON RICH

Oraibi, was settled in the twelfth century and is the oldest continuously occupied town in the United States. Their religious ceremonies, including the famous snake dance in which men hold live rattlesnakes in their teeth, all center around the traditional kiva. Some of their farming methods were probably used long ago in the volcanic ash near Sunset Crater. And their pottery, weaving, and jewelry, though highly individualistic, are evocative of the work of the Pueblo craftsmen.

The Havasupai, inhabiting Havasu or Cataract Canyon near the west end of Grand Canyon National Park, are thought to be descended from the ancient Cohonina—which if true would apply also to their close relatives the Hualpai (or Hualapai or Walapai) who occupy a large reservation farther west on the south rim of Grand Canyon. The Havasupai's is a beautiful home: a green oasis cradled among brilliant red cliffs, well watered by a permanent creek that tumbles in great waterfalls into turquoise pools which give the tribe its name, "People of the Blue-Green Water." It may also be the most isolated home of any tribe in the country: it is accessible only by steep horse or foot trails at the end of many miles of dirt road. The Havasupai as a result have not changed much since they befriended Father Garcés in 1776.

The impoverished Paiutes, living today on the Kanab Indian Reservation north of the Grand Canyon and on other small reservations in Utah and Nevada, speak a language somewhat similar to that of the Hopi, and while not descended from the ancient Kayenta, might be regarded as their distant kin. But the best-known Indian tribe of the Grand Canyon country—and, with sixty thousand members, the biggest in the United States—only penetrated northern Arizona from New Mexico in historic times. The Navajo, like the Apache, belong to the Athapascan family, the principal body of which is found in Canada, and they still talk of a traditional home to the north.

Everything about the Navajos' modern way of life is adopted, and yet, as Krutch writes, "they could not be more loyal to it were its traditions as old as the tribe itself."

Until the Spanish came they had no sheep or horses. They stole their first stock and turned to herding with such dedication that their sheep, goats, and horses have seriously overgrazed the range. They knew nothing of weaving or working silver. With their superb blankets and jewelry they are now among the most famous craftsmen of the Southwest. Their dome-shaped mud hogans dot the landscape to the east of the Marble Gorge as if they had grown out of the earth like mushrooms. The women standing before them in their velvet blouses and long voluminous skirts; the children herding sheep by the roadside; the occasional lone Navajo riding his pony across the sagebrush from nowhere to nowhere—all these seem as much a part of this ancient land as do its rocks themselves.

Clouds are playing in the canyon to-day. Sometimes they roll down in great masses, filling the gorge with gloom; sometimes they hang aloft from wall to wall and cover the canyon with a roof of impending storm, and we can peer long distances up and down this canyon corridor, with its cloud-roof overhead, its walls of black granite, and its river bright with the sheen of broken waters. Then a gust of wind sweeps down a side gulch and, making a rift in the clouds, reveals the blue heavens, and a stream of sunlight pours in. Then the clouds drift away into the distance, and hang around crags and peaks and pinnacles and towers and walls, and cover them with a mantle that lifts from time to time and sets them all in sharp relief. Then baby clouds creep out of side canyons, glide around points, and creep back again into more distant gorges. Then clouds arrange in strata across the canyon, with intervening vista views to cliffs and rocks beyond. The clouds are children of the heavens, and when they play among the rocks they lift them to the region above.

JOHN WESLEY POWELL

PHILIP HYDE: Sunset, downriver from Nankoweap Creek

6. Hance Rapid

WE ABANDONED the cliff ruins to the ghosts of the Ancient Ones, stumbled and skidded down the steep slope to the beach, and soon pushed off onto the river. We entered a straight aisle of the Canyon three miles long, between the Desert Façade on our left and Nankoweap Mesa on our right. Low taluses and ledges of the green Bright Angel shale formed the foundations of the walls, and the river swung from side to side between banks grown thick with mesquite. After an hour we stopped on the right at the head of Kwagunt Rapid. Judging from the cut willows along the bank this area must be teeming with beaver. Such signs, as well as tracks, had been frequent in Marble Gorge, but we had never had so much as a glimpse of the animals. One evening only, as we approached the proposed dam site, we had heard a report like the crack of a pistol—the unmistakable slap of a beaver's tail on the water.

Kwagunt gave us a tricky, twisting run, with the boatmen straining to quarter between the main waves and heavy laterals, but we sailed through in good order. Another two hours, marked by smaller rapids and riffles and an increasingly heavy head wind, and we were suddenly out of the Marble Gorge. The Colorado river curved sharply to the right, and on the left, issuing from a canyon almost as grand as the big river's, the Little Colorado joined it. Much of the time, the Little Colorado is a beautiful turquoise blue, and the line where its waters meet the main river's is as sharp as the border between two colors in a flag. I had looked forward to this contrast but was disappointed: the Little Colorado was in flood, its waters even redder and more turbid than the Colorado's.

"We are now ready to start on our way down the Great Unknown," Powell had written of this point. We were ready also, but it looked as if the Great Unknown did not welcome our prying. The wind came swirling up the Canyon in long, heavy gusts. Plumes of sand streamed from the beaches below the dark ledges of Tapeats sandstone, and mixed with stinging spume from the river, forcing us to keep our heads down. Between the heavier blows we stole looks at the scenery. Here the Canyon was wide open, and we could see more sky than at any time since leaving Lee's Ferry. Rounding a bend where the river turned left we looked down the jagged face of the Palisades of the Desert to the South Rim, ten miles away and nearly a mile above us, and we could just make out the Desert View tower. After the regularity of the forms in the Marble Gorge the scene seemed jumbled at first. Asymmetrical buttes and bluffs rose above the river to our right. The horizontal strata were replaced in the foreground by the bent and tilted planes of the Grand Canyon Series, and volcanic sills and mounds added to the confusion.

The wind grew so strong that it overcame the river's current, and the boatmen had to pull hard not to be blown upstream. Harassed by the flying sand and spray, we all were relieved when Pat Reilly spotted a relatively sheltered cove on the left bank and announced we would make camp there. As we landed Bill Jones noticed some fresh coyote tracks in the wet sand along the shore—so fresh that it seemed likely the animal had watched us approach before he vanished. Our food at supper was liberally seasoned with sand, but the wind was abating, and after dinner the overcast cleared and the setting sun gloriously spotlighted the cliffs above our heads.

Pat Reilly recalled a hike he had taken on another trip, up Lava Canyon across the river. He had seen Indian ruins and petroglyphs, as well as the remains of a pre-Prohibition still that had operated safely out of the reach of the law. Not far from our camp was the old Horsethieves' Ford, across which rustlers used to drive stock stolen from the Mormons for sale in the Flagstaff area, and return with horses stolen around Flagstaff for sale to the Mormons. There are several stories of lost mines in this area, including one said to have been worked by Lee while he was in hiding. About three miles downstream from us was the end of the Tanner Trail, built by Seth Tanner, who worked a prospect nearby. Undaunted by climate or topography, prospectors investigated the farthest recesses of the Grand Canyon in the late 1800's. Silver, copper, asbestos and other mines were opened, though none made any fortunes for their owners. Most of the seldom-traveled trails leading into the Canyon today were old Indian trails rebuilt by these hardy miners and several bear their names—Tanner Trail, Hance Trail, Bass Trail, Boucher Trail.

The next day dawned windy and raw, and a veil of rain or snow shrouded the south rim west of Desert View. The river had dropped two feet during the night, and Pat Reilly and Martin Litton feared—rightly as it turned out—that exposed rocks might give us trouble in some of the rapids. But all went well enough at first. We had good, exhilarating runs through Lava Canyon and Tanner Canyon rapids, and landed above Unkar Creek Rapid at midmorning. Situated in the lower half of a long S-shaped bend of the river, Unkar was a seething cauldron of mad waves as the current dashed itself against a high sheer cliff of red shale on the left side, then rebounded with unspent violence. Leaving the boatmen to decide on a course through the rapid, the rest of us scattered over the wide sloping bench on the right of the river. It was thickly littered with potsherds, including one particularly colorful one with two shades of red separated by a band of orange. A goodly population of Indians once farmed along Unkar Creek, and the circles of rocks we found here and there may have been the foundations of their pithouses. Humble dwellings they were, but even the mightiest of men's buildings would have been dwarfed in this setting. The cliffs of Cape Final, eight thousand feet in elevation, loomed above us to the north. The stepped pyramids of Solomon Temple, Rama Shrine, Vishnu Temple, Freya Castle, Jupiter, Venus, and Apollo Temples, each a mountain in its own right, formed the wings of a gigantic amphitheater. I thought of Napoleon's exhortation to his troops before the Battle of the Pyramids: "Soldats, songez que, du haut de ces pyramides, quarante siècles vous contemplent." Only from *these* pyramids, more nearly forty *thousand* centuries looked down upon us.

Despite its ferocious appearance, Unkar Rapid proved easy. We "cheated" it to the right, avoiding the bigger water and staying well away from the menacing cliff. We were feeling cocky an hour later as we piled into Seventy-five Mile Rapid. Pat Reilly and Martin Litton went ahead. Patience sat up on the forepeak of the *Lucky Pierre* with Bill Jones' movie camera, filming the first two boats; I sat relaxed, watching Litton expertly take on the rather monstrous waves; Jones handled the oars with non-chalance, all the while singing as if he had been a gondolier on the Grand Canal in Venice. Suddenly—sssssSSSSSSSSWHOOOOOM!—a mountain of water came hissing up, smashed against our bow, and drenched us to the skin. "Guess I'd better get serious," Bill Jones shouted half-seriously. Just then I saw Martin the Imperturbable begin to row as if he meant it. I soon realized why, as he barely avoided a rock that lay just below the

surface. We too were fast bearing down on that rock, and seeing it Bill Jones pulled hard against the oars—too late. Over the rock we swept, plunging broadside into the hole below. I had a flash impression of water pouring over the gunwale, of Bill Jones toppling over the side, of the boat turning like a turkey on a spit, then all went cold and dark. In that murky, churning water I did not know which direction was up—but my life-jacket took care of that and after what felt like a very long moment I bobbed to the surface. The overturned boat was just ahead; with two or three strokes I reached it and grabbed hold of the gunwale. I saw Jones hanging on to the bow and my wife emerged at my right shoulder from under the boat, still holding the movie camera.

We were being swept along at a good clip, and as the boat rose and fell in the tail waves of the rapid we rose and fell with it. The sensation was exciting, and had the season been later and the water less cold I should have wished that the rapid were a mile long. A scene from the movie "In Which We Serve" flashed through my mind, wherein sailors from a sunken British destroyer sit in a rubber raft singing "Roll Out the Barrel." I started to sing "Cool Green Water," which I thought appropriate, but no chorus developed. Then the *Portolá* and *Susie Too* drew up alongside and we were fished out of the water. Pat Reilly, with the *Lucky Pierre* in tow, landed on the left in a cove at the foot of the rapid, and Martin Litton beached the *Portolá* alongside. Ardis Hyde quickly built a fire, and soon some hot coffee had thawed us out. The *Lucky Pierre* was righted and bailed out, and the gear re-stowed. We were safe, the boat was undamaged, and we could take delight in an incident which would provide us henceforth with a splendid conversation piece. We had lost one thing in that rapid, however—and that was our cockiness. The Colorado had taught us a lesson.

Thus it was with renewed respect that we stood an hour later, after an uneventful run down from Seventy-five Mile Rapid, on the boulder-strewn bank studying the awesome fury of Hance Rapid. Roaring by between us and the slope of brilliant red Hakatai shale on the opposite side, Hance looked longer, bigger and rougher than any we had yet come to, a mess of exposed or just-submerged rocks, exploding haystacks and "rooster tails." After a long, sober war council Pat Reilly decided to tackle it in the morning, hoping that the wind would have died and the sun be shining by then. The boatmen would run solo, the boats being more maneuverable and better balanced without the weight of the passengers. Secretly grateful for this reprieve, we all went about our

... They pushed off into the real Colorado, the old man himself, an awesome river wide and deep and the color of cocoa. The thousand yards of serene current visible from the junction lengthened out to three miles. Then rapids, bad ones, in quick succession. They portaged and lined when they could, ran when there seemed no other choice.

WALLACE STEGNER

CLYDE CHILDRESS: Lining Granite Falls Rapid, Mile 93.5

CLYDE THOMAS: Lining Lava Falls, Mile 179.4

CLYDE CHILDRESS: Serpentine Rapid

All across the great barren Marble Canyon Platform which stretches north of the river from the monoclinal eastern flank of the Kaibab to the angle of the Vermilion Cliffs, abrupt gorges come in, cut by runoff waters from the higher country. Badger Creek and Soap Creek and other lesser watercourses come in by canyons as deep as the river's own, and every junction is piled with the boulders of flash floods. Every junction is a rapid; the prevailing strike of the beds is upstream, a condition which is a maker of rapids as surely as hard rock and lateral gorges are. And the Colorado now is a great stream, but squeezed into a narrow frothing channel that reflects every summer shower by sharp rises. Between high and low water in parts of the canyon there is a vertical difference of a hundred feet. At low water the rocks are deadly, at high water the waves toss a boat like a chip. And they are waves of a peculiar ferocity, for they are not ocean waves, where the water remains in place and only the form passes on. Here the form remains and the water passes on, and it goes like fire engines, with a roar that trembles the rocks, and in flood the water itself is heavy with red silt.

WALLACE STEGNER

CLYDE THOMAS: Lava Falls, also called Vulcan Rapid

business, choosing campsites, taking notes, photographing or exploring. I hiked a short distance up Red Canyon, through which the Hance Trail came down from the South Rim. Half hidden among the mesquites near the mouth of Red Canyon were the tumbled remains of what seemed to have been a wooden cabin, a dilapidated fence, parts of a cast iron stove, and rusted pots and pans. This once had been John Hance's tourist camp.

"Captain" Hance he called himself—but since he parried all questions about his past with the statement, "I do not like ancient history," the nature of his commission was difficult to ascertain. He came to the South Rim about 1881, built a cabin on the rim just east of Grandview Point, and worked an asbestos mine in the bottom of the Canyon to which he constructed a trail. But the mine, which did not pay because of the prohibitive cost of getting the asbestos up to the rim, became Hance's excuse rather than his reason for remaining at the Grand Canyon. The truth was that he loved the Canyon. When tourists started arriving by stagecoach from Flagstaff in the late eighteen hundreds Hance put them up at his camp on the rim, and delighted in leading them down his trail to the river. He also delighted in telling tall stories, such as of snowshoeing across to the North Rim on top of the fog.

William Wallace Bass, who had built an aerial tramway across the Colorado and planted an orchard on the north side of the river, also ran a tourist camp on the South Rim, near Havasupai Point. The first hotel was built at Grandview Point in 1892 by P. D. "Pete" Barry, who had a copper mine on Horseshoe Mesa and who also improved the old Indian trail to Indian Gardens, along the Bright Angel geologic fault. After the turn of the century William Randolph Hearst bought these properties, and planned to exploit the growing tourist possibilities of the Grand Canyon. But he had competition. The Santa Fe railway extended a line from Williams to the South Rim, and in 1904 the Fred Harvey Company, in conjunction with the Santa Fe, built the El Tovar Hotel—hiring John Hance to entertain the guests. Hearst had no railroad leading to his back porch and was forced to abandon his schemes.

Far down the Canyon, on Diamond Creek, another hotel was operating. In the early years of this century it looked as if the Grand Canyon might in time become another commercialized vacationers' mecca, dotted with resorts and health spas and handrailed trails. But there were those who had a different vision for the Grand Canyon. This, they believed, was no place to be exploited for private profit by a few individuals. The Grand Canyon

was one of the glories of the Nation, and should *belong* to the Nation and be preserved by it unblemished for the inspiration of the present and future generations of Americans.

In 1887, Senator Benjamin Harrison of Indiana introduced a bill to make the Grand Canyon a National Park, fifty-six miles long and sixty-nine miles wide. But opposition from Arizona killed the bill. As President of the United States, Harrison in 1893 established the Grand Canyon Forest Preserve. But this still left the area open to exploitation by mining and lumbering and grazing interests. Ten years later, President Theodore Roosevelt visited the Grand Canyon for the first time. No public figure of his day displayed a deeper feeling for America's natural heritage. And no man before or since in a position of political power ever did so much to preserve this heritage. On the occasion of his visit, Roosevelt made a speech which expresses the core of the conservationist creed:

"In the Grand Canyon, Arizona has a natural wonder which, so far as I know, is in kind absolutely unparalleled throughout the rest of the world. I want to ask you to do one thing in connection with it in your own interest and in the interest of the country—to keep this great wonder of nature as it now is. I was delighted to learn of the wisdom of the Santa Fe railroad people in deciding not to build their hotel on the brink of the Canyon. I hope you will not have a building of any kind, not a summer cottage, a hotel or anything else, to mar the wonderful grandeur, the sublimity, the great loveliness and beauty of the Canyon. Leave it as it is. You cannot improve on it. The ages have been at work on it, and man can only mar it. What you can do is to keep it for your children, your children's children, and for all who come after you, as one of the great sights which every American if he can travel at all should see. We have gotten past the stage, my fellow citizens, when we are to be pardoned if we treat any part of our country as something to be skinned for two or three years for the use of the present generation, whether it be the forest, the water, the scenery. Whatever it is, handle it so that your children's children will get the benefit of it."

T. R. was not the sort of man to make fine-sounding speeches and let it go at that. In 1908, by a stroke of the pen he proclaimed the Grand Canyon a National Monument. Still this did not give the Canyon the full protection of law, since a future President could unmake the Monument just as easily. Nor did it discourage the many interests which sought to utilize the Grand Canyon for private gain. In 1909, a bill was introduced in Congress entitling Ralph H. Cameron to build a scenic railway along the Canyon rim, but the bill created an uproar and failed. There were schemes to run sightseeing cars across the Canyon on wire cables; others proposed to utilize its waters for power. Innumerable mining claims were filed, some of them bona fide, but many intended only to delay the establishment of a National Park.

For a decade opposition by these interests, by stockmen, and by the State of Arizona frustrated attempts to pass a Grand Canyon National Park bill. And as a result of these tactics the bill which finally was approved by Congress and became law in 1919 set aside a much smaller area than that which had been proposed in 1910 by the American Scenic and Historic Preservation Society. As finally established, the Grand Canyon National Park included—and includes—only a small portion of the total Canyon. It is about fifty air miles long from east to west and twenty-five miles wide from north to south, and contains only 73 miles of the Colorado River's winding 280 mile course through the Canyon. The southern boundary zigzags along just back of the rim, except at the western end of the park where it cuts across the base of Great Thumb Mesa and skirts around the enclave of the Havasupai Indian Reservation, reaching the river near the mouth of Havasu Creek. The eastern boundary includes only the last nine miles of the Marble Gorge from Little Nankoweap Creek to the mouth of the Little Colorado—and only the west bank of the river at that. It jogs east three miles up the Little Colorado, and cuts due south by Cedar Mountain to a point four miles southeast of Desert View, where it joins the southern boundary.

The northern line of the Park is even more capricious. It begins at the mouth of Little Nankoweap Creek, strikes the North Rim about two miles north of Point Imperial, thence heads generally westward to include the southernmost extremity of the Kaibab Plateau—an area insufficient, as we shall see later, to guarantee the survival of one of the rarest, prettiest, and zoölogically most interesting of Grand Canyon animals. The gerrymandered boundary hits the rim again in the vicinity of the detached mass of the Powell Plateau, follows the very brink of the rim for a few miles to the north and west, then cuts right down to the river at the mouth of Tapeats Creek. For the rest of the way to Havasu Creek, the river forms the northern and western boundary of the Park. Between Tapeats Creek and Kanab Creek, a distance of eleven miles, the north bank of the Colorado lies in the Kaibab National Forest. Grazing, lumbering, mining, hunting, the building of waterworks are all theoretically sanctioned under the Forest Service's multiple use for-

mula, with the result that the wilderness character of this portion of the Canyon has no legal protection.

West of Kanab Creek stretches the Grand Canyon National Monument. Established in 1932, the Monument comprises 314 square miles and includes, as its primary raison d'être, the unusual vestiges of volcanic activity in the neighborhood of Toroweap. Most of the Monument is on the north side of the Canyon, where it adjoins the river for 39 miles, but it also projects to the south of the river, between the National Park and the Hualpai Indian Reservation.

The Grand Canyon thus is a fragmented entity. Between Lee's Ferry and Lake Mead the right bank of the Colorado lies successively in Bureau of Land Management lands, in the National Forest, in the National Park, in the National Forest, in the National Monument, and finally in the Lake Mead National Recreation Area. The left bank belongs first to the Navajo Indian Reservation, then to the National Park, the National Monument, the Hualpai Indian Reservation, and again the Lake Mead National Recreation Area. Therein lies chaos. For only within the bounds of the Park and Monument must Roosevelt's admonition to "Leave it as it is" be more or less strictly observed.

The very immensity of the Canyon has protected it so far from the impact of heavy human use. Even in the Park, you can walk a short distance from any of the marked viewpoints, and have the Grand Canyon for your own—which it is: as a National Park, it is *your* property. Or, to be more exact, *almost* your own. For that raven, soaring out there contemptuous of the void, those pretty ground squirrels scuttering about the rocks at your feet, have property rights that precede yours. Only in the National Parks, unfortunately, is the wildlife's Lebensraum given recognition, and their territorial rights awarded full protection of law. And this protection extends to the cougar, rattlesnake and scorpion, as much as to the deer, squirrel or bird.

Solitude, inasmuch as it aids contemplation, is almost essential for an appreciation of the Canyon. It is simply too vast, too overwhelming, seemingly too confusing to register on your mind at first sight. Asleep in the blinding glare of the noon hours, it appears strangely amorphous, almost unreal. Often a thick blue haze fills it to the brim, muting the colors of the rocks, blurring the shapes of the promontories and buttes, foreshortening the distances. You feel disoriented, your sense of scale lost. If your perch happens to give you a glimpse of the Colorado deep in the Inner Gorge, you will find it difficult, as did Cárdenas and his men, to accept the fact that it is a major river and not a muddy brook.

But just sit and wait a while. Clouds may soon begin to gather, and as their shadows course across the gulf individual features expand into relief. In this phantasmagoria of light and shadow you may begin to discern a logic in the forms. The ground plan of the Canyon is infinitely varied, with jutting points and deep bays, isolated, buttressed buttes, and crenelated castles. Yet the vertical plan is everywhere consistent. Above the dark rock of the Inner Gorge the same layers everywhere rise one above the other, each with its individual profile— a wide, green slope, a sheer red wall, a succession of red slopes and cliffs, a straight buff-colored cliff topped by an abrupt talus and a grayish-white precipice. Some of the buttes and temples lack one or more of the upper layers, which have weathered away over the ages, but their vertical plan too is consistent as far as it goes. The Canyon is like a passacaglia—a constantly recurring theme underlies the variations.

"Throughout the afternoon," Dutton writes, "the prospect has been gradually growing clearer. The haze has relaxed its steely glare and has changed to a veil of transparent blue. Slowly the myriads of details have come out and the walls are flecked with lines of minute tracery, forming a diaper of light and shade. . . . All things seem to grow in beauty, power and dimensions. What was grand before has become majestic, the majestic becomes sublime, and, ever expanding and developing, the sublime passes beyond the reach of our faculties and becomes transcendent. The colors have come back. Inherently rich and strong, though not superlative under ordinary light, they now begin to display an adventitious brilliancy. The western sky is all aflame. The scattered banks of cloud and wavy cirrus have caught the waning splendor, and shine with orange and crimson. Broad slant beams of yellow light, shot through the glory-rifts, fall on turret and tower, on pinnacled crest and winding ledge, suffusing them with a radiance less fulsome, but akin to that which flames in the western clouds. The summit band is brilliant yellow; the next below is pale rose. But the grand expanse within is a deep, luminous, resplendent red. The climax has now come. The blaze of sunlight poured over an illimitable surface of glowing red is flung back into the gulf, and, commingling with the blue haze, turns it into a sea of purple of most imperial hue—so rich, so strong, so pure that it makes the heart ache and the throat tighten. However vast the magnitudes, however majestic the forms, or sumptuous the decoration, it is in these kingly colors that the highest glory of the Grand Canyon is revealed.

"At length the sun sinks and the colors cease to burn.

The abyss lapses back into repose. But its glory mounts upward and diffuses itself in the sky above. Long streamers of rosy light, rayed out from the west, cross the firmament and converge again in the east, ending in a pale rosy arch, which rises like a low aurora just above the eastern horizon. Below it is the dead gray shadow of the world. Higher and higher climbs the arch, followed by the darkening pall of gray, and as it ascends it fades and disappears, leaving no color except the afterglow of the western clouds and the lusterless red of the chasm below. Within the abyss the darkness gathers. Gradually the shades deepen and ascend, hiding the opposite wall and enveloping the great temples. For a few moments the summits of these majestic piles seem to float upon a sea of blackness, then vanish in the darkness, and, wrapped in the impenetrable mantle of the night, they await the glory of the coming dawn."

Purple prose? Romantic exaggeration? Only to the reader who has never witnessed the scene Dutton describes. There is perhaps no spectacle on earth as poignant and sublime as the Grand Canyon at sunset. Still, viewed from any point on either rim, it remains mainly a spectacle. You are but an outsider, looking in. You can stand on the shore watching the surf sweep in and gain some knowledge of the ocean, but it is not the intimate knowledge of the sailor who goes to sea. So too with the Grand Canyon. Only by stepping off the rim and descending toward the river can you identify, if only temporarily, with the Canyon world. Only by looking up at its formidable cliffs, at the rim which seems to retreat before you as you climb, like a mocking mirage, can you develop your own perception of its real dimensions. And only by journeying all the way to the river, where it swirls and rumbles and still carves its way through some of the oldest rocks on earth, can you fully appreciate the work of the two great architects of the Grand Canyon, time and the flowing river.

Cognizant of this, the National Park Service encourages tourists to take the mule trips down the Bright Angel and Kaibab trails, to Phantom Ranch in the bottom of the Canyon. The mules, with their seeming indifference to the precipices along the trails, cause their riders some trepidation, though the animals are statistically a far safer mode of conveyance than the vehicles that brought the tourists to the Park. The hardier visitor may prefer to don a backpack and hike down these trails to the river. This has advantages over the mule ride: he can set his own pace, stopping wherever he wants, to take photographs or botanize or study a fossil's imprint in a trailside rock. A few, still more adventurous and expert in the art of reading topographic maps, explore trails into the Canyon that are no longer maintained, such as the Tanner, Hance, Grandview, Hermit, and Bass trails from the South Rim, or the Thunder River and Shinumo (or North Bass), and Nankoweap trails on the North Rim. Solitude on these trails is not only easy to find—it is practically inescapable.

And then there is J. Harvey Butchart. As I walked back to our beach that afternoon, after poking around the ruins of Hance's camp, I at once spotted Dr. Butchart, who stood talking with Pat Reilly. I was not surprised—the meeting had been scheduled before the start of our boat trip—still it was somewhat startling to have another human materialize out of the wilderness, and stand there matter-of-factly as if this were the corner of First and Main streets. Dr. Butchart had driven up that morning from Flagstaff, where he heads the Mathematics Department at Arizona State College. He had started down the Tanner Trail from Lipan Point, then had turned left off the trail to seek a possible new route down the face of the Redwall; he had found one, and later had discovered a new way down the cliff of Tapeats sandstone as well. Reaching the river he had turned west and followed its bank, floating down part of the way on his inflated air mattress, and had arrived at our camp on schedule and apparently unwearied. In the morning, he would climb the vertical mile to the rim by the Hance Trail.

This, for Harvey Butchart, was only a mildly strenuous hike. Well up in his fifties, this small, spare, wiry man could set a pace which would leave much younger men rubber-kneed and gasping for breath. He only followed trails when it was convenient to do so. In years of Canyon hiking, on weekends and vacations, he had climbed twenty-eight of its temples and buttes, and eighteen of these were first ascents. I once told him that he must know the Canyon's inner fastness as well as the native bighorn sheep or wild burros did. But when he showed me his topographic maps crisscrossed in ink with the routes of his various hikes, I realized I had underestimated him. No individual bighorn or burro ever had traveled so much of the Grand Canyon.

Of course there are not many of Harvey Butchart's kind. And, realizing this, there are quite a few men who would be happy to reduce the Grand Canyon National Park's 1,100 square miles by excluding those areas which have seldom, or never, been trodden by man. But these people miss the point. It is not only for Harvey Butchart and a few others like him that hundreds of thousands of acres of Grand Canyon wilderness have been set aside. It is not only for the sake of a few white water enthusiasts—perhaps nine hundred since Powell's day—that proposals to dam or divert the flow of the Colorado River have been and are being vociferously opposed. The Canyon's vast splendor—and the exciting knowledge that it is still wild, just as nature made it and not as re-made by man—are the patrimony of all Americans, even of those, to paraphrase Stegner, who only drive up to the rim of the Canyon and simply sit and look. Even if they have neither the time nor the physical stamina to descend into it, they can let their imaginations roam as they look into its depths, see the ages at work on it, picture the interplay of natural forces that are still fashioning it and the lives of the wild things that are its citizens. The images may not always jibe with reality, but these visitors will be the richer for the experience.

The American's right—you might say birthright—to such an experience was confirmed by Congress in 1916 when it passed the National Parks Act. This has remained the basic law under which some of the finest remnants of the country's fast-disappearing natural beauty have been preserved. As the Act states it, "the fundamental purpose of the . . . parks . . . is to conserve the scenery and the natural and historic objects and the wildlife therein, and to provide for the enjoyment of the same in such manner and by such means as will leave them unimpaired for the enjoyment of future generations."

Unimpaired is the key word in the Act. So far, it has been interpreted as meaning that the parks' natural values have precedence over all others. Hunting, grazing, mining, lumbering must be rigidly excluded. With unfortunate exceptions, airfields and speedboat ramps are to be sought elsewhere. So are public golf links, ski lifts, and the like. Access roads and public accommodations—again with unhappy exceptions—are kept as simple as possible and designed by and large to harmonize with the contours and character of the landscape.

In Grand Canyon National Park, the Park Service has steadily opposed would-be profiteers who would build a funicular to the river for visitors who possess neither the energy to ride mules or hike into the Canyon nor the powers of imagination which could compensate for it. They have discouraged those who would like a direct highway between the South and North Rim hotels. And they did fight against the dam and diversion projects, which would either rob the river of its water or back a reservoir into the Monument and Park—until they were compelled by higher powers to maintain a glum silence.

7. Granite Gorge

DAWN FILLED the Canyon with golden light and gave promise of a warm, clear day. The wind had died down to a light breeze that ruffled the new acacia-like leaves of the mesquites, alive with gnatcatchers and yellow warblers. The sun awakened the rich colors of the rocks, and alchemized the iridescence of the hummingbirds' plumage. It was a morning when nature flaunted her many-splendored beauty like a peacock spreading its dazzling tail.

After bidding farewell to Harvey Butchart, who quick-stepped up Red Canyon about seven o'clock to meet his noon rendezvous at the rim, I walked to the shore and stood looking at Hance Rapid, watching the rooster tails dance in the sun, and listening to the booming voice of the great river of the West. Not great in volume: the Columbia has at least twelve times the Colorado's flow. But great in nearly every other respect: in its length —nearly two thousand miles from its source in the Colorado Rockies to its mouth at the Gulf of California; in the size of its watershed—244,000 square miles of lofty ranges, high, semiarid plateaus, and sun-scorched deserts; great also in the magnificence of the land through which it flows and which it has helped to shape.

This was our seventh day on the river. For a week we had been conscious of it at all times; it had provided both the route and the motive power for our journey through the canyon wilderness; its noise had filled our ears by day, and had lulled us to sleep at night; its changing aspects had dictated our moods—serenity in the quieter stretches, exultation in the rapids. Increasingly I had found myself ascribing these moods to the river itself, endowing it with the personality of an animate being. This was nonsense, of course—the Colorado was as incapable of serenity or anger as the rocks of its Canyon walls. In fact, to be accurate I should amend my statement that the river had taught us a lesson in Seventy-five Mile Rapid—we had taught ourselves a lesson, by paying the price of our carelessness, and the Colorado had been only a tool like a blackboard in a schoolroom. Still the illusion was tenacious that the river had a will and a character of its own. This illusion was an essential part of the romance and the challenge of the flowing river, and would be utterly destroyed, with the romance and the challenge, if and when the proposed dams were built.

As I watched the tumultuous waters of the rapid at my feet, I wondered how the boatmen would fare running solo. They would have an exciting ride, that much I could foresee, and I regretted having to sit this one out. Oddly enough, if our upset had inspired us with greater caution it also had put an end to any morbid apprehensions we might have had. The water and air were not yet warm enough to deliberately swim a rapid, as members of boat parties occasionally do in the summer. But a dunking, we now felt sure, could mean little more than a passing discomfort and some loss of time.

As it turned out, Pat Reilly, Bill Jones and Martin Litton peeled off one after the other and ran Hance almost without trouble, although Bill Jones had a brief contretemps when his boat hung up momentarily on a rock. We passengers climbed aboard at the foot of the rapid, and almost immediately we entered the famous Granite Gorge. Minutes later we were tumbling through Sockdologer Rapid—a long, long chute of frenzied waves with a total fall of nineteen feet. Patience and I were obliged by the way the *Lucky Pierre* was loaded to sit facing upstream, but Bill Jones' running commentary kept us informed of what to expect. "Watch your weight, watch your balance," he warned. "Here comes a big one! . . . Here comes another big one! . . . Here comes the biggest one!" Then we were among the tail waves, with the boat rocking rhythmically like a hobby horse.

The aspect of the Canyon, or rather of its Inner Gorge, had changed dramatically. Gone were the straight, horizontally banded walls of the Marble Gorge, gone was the openness of the sky below the junction with the Little Colorado. The inner canyon now formed a narrow V more than a thousand feet deep. The Vishnu schist that made its walls was in places dark as coal. Its planes angled sharply upward, and the rock had a twisted and fractured and tortured appearance—tortured by the unimaginable heat and pressure that had metamorphosed the original sedimentary rocks. Wide and thin dikes of pink granite, sparkling with quartz and mica, writhed through the schist. At the water's edge the latter was beautifully fluted and polished, with a texture much like carved ebony. The schist looked immensely ancient, as indeed it was. Few exposed rocks on earth rival it in age.

The thunder of the rapids reverberated from the walls of the narrow gorge. At the mouth of every tributary canyon was a fan of boulders washed down during flash floods. These boulders constricted and obstructed the channel of the river, resulting in a rapid or at least a riffle. Grapevine matched Sockdologer in its sound and fury. Eighty-three Mile Rapid amply justified its nickname, "The Little Bastard." Then Clear Creek Rapid, Zoroaster Rapid, and the excitement was over for the day. Rowing steadily in the warmth of the afternoon, we had magnificent views of Isis Temple high ahead of us, its symmetrical shape and colorful sunlit layers contrasting with the gnarled, Stygian rocks of the Gorge. We rounded a bend, and saw the river gauging station, with its twin cable cars hung across the river, and beyond it the Kaibab suspension bridge, a one-mule-wide structure connecting the North and South Kaibab Trails.

Once more, after eight days, we were in touch with civilization—a remote outpost of it, to be sure—but not a soul was around to give us a fanfare as our little boats tied up at the beach above Bright Angel Creek. Walking over to Phantom Ranch we passed the campground, which held interesting memories for me. I had spent a night there two months earlier after hiking down the Kaibab Trail with a group of astronauts and U. S. Geological Survey experts. The U.S.G.S. men had lectured us along the way about the geology of the Canyon. And what had fired my imagination nearly as much as the story of the Canyon was the way an instructor would say to the astronauts, "You won't find this formation on the moon, but you might look for something like it on Mars." This was said, and accepted, as matter-of-factly as if the instructor had remarked, "You won't find this in Burma but you might run into it in Brazil."

In his *Ancient Landscapes of the Grand Canyon Region*, geologist McKee writes: "From the rim of Grand Canyon one not only looks down through tremendous space, but also through time, glimpsing the record of vast ages, measurable not in centuries but in millions and even hundreds of millions of years." That hike with the astronauts had been a journey back into time. And so had our boat traverse. Each new layer of rock that had risen at the water's edge had represented an earlier chapter in the history of the planet. And one of the marvels of the Canyon is that more such chapters are revealed here than anywhere else on earth.

The Grand Canyon story begins two billion years ago.

And as with all ancient history the beginnings are part conjecture. The region was probably a shallow, subsiding marine basin, in which there had built up great horizontal deposits of sand and mud. These deposits are still seen in the Canyon's Inner Gorge, though no longer recognizable for what they once were. For as the earth's inner core slowly cooled and contracted, tremendous pressures were set up in its outer shell as it sought to accommodate itself to the shrinking sphere within. Gradually the earth's crust wrinkled like the skin of a drying prune. In the Grand Canyon region, great mountains slowly rose that may have rivaled today's Himalayas. The original sedimentary layers were tilted into nearly vertical planes, and the rocks themselves compressed and heated until they became the dark, enormously hard Vishnu schist. Molten rock squeezed up through fissures in the schist, crystallizing into granite underground and spewing forth as lava where it reached the surface.

This ancient landscape must have been bleak beyond description. No living thing, if any lived, had dared to venture from the ocean's womb. The whistling of the wind, the rolling of thunder, the splashing of rain, the roar of a landslide were the only sounds, and even they were wasted since there were no ears to hear them. No moss or lichen softened the edges of the naked rocks; the mountains wore no green mantle of trees; and nothing moved across their flanks except the shadows of the clouds.

What nature hath put together, nature will put asunder. Just as slowly as orogenic forces had built the Archean mountains, the winds and rains and streams and frosts tore them down again, until, one billion years ago, the Grand Canyon region was reduced to an almost level plain. Then, in a great crustal ebb tide, the plain subsided beneath the sea. A second great era of building and erosion was set to begin—the Late Precambrian or Proterozoic Era, during which the Grand Canyon's Algonkian System of rocks was laid down.

As the geologist would say, the lowest Algonkian layer, the Hotauta conglomerate, rests "unconformably" on the underlying Archean schist and granite—in other words, the more recent layer does not rest directly on the original surface of the older. There is no physical separation between the two strata—but there is a gap in time of 500,000,000 years. Before such figures the mind reels. However, there is another gap between Archean and Algonkian, which we are better able to grasp. The Archean rock is barren of any evidence of life. But in the Bass limestone, directly above the Hotauta, are found the earliest traces of living things, reefs built up by the secretions of one-celled plants known as algae. And this leap from the lifeless to the live transcends any gap of time.

For a considerable portion of the Proterozoic Era's 500,000,000 years, the Grand Canyon region was buried under shallow seas, with perhaps brief periods of emergence. During this time thousands of feet of sediment were laid down—seven thousand feet in the Unkar Group of Bass limestone, Hakatai shale, Shinumo quartzite and Dox sandstone; five thousand feet in the Chuar group now exposed east of the Butte Fault near the mouth of the Little Colorado. Then, once again, the crustal tide changed. Great fault-block mountains, similar to today's Grand Tetons, were thrust up thousands of feet into the sky. The Algonkian strata were sharply tilted—hence another term for them, the Wedge Series, to differentiate them from the Vertical Series below and the Horizontal Series of the Canyon's upper layers. These mountains were just as grim as their predecessors: there definitely was life on earth by then, but it was all at sea.

A second great period of erosion next set in. So complete was this denudation that the mountains were reduced to a scattering of low hills, rising a few hundred feet at most above an arid peneplain. From much of this plain the Algonkian covering was completely stripped, with the result that when the Cambrian Sea moved into the area its first sediments were deposited directly on the Archean rock. This contact of the Tapeats sandstone, 500,000,000 years old, with the 2,000,000,000-year-old Vishnu schist is known as the Great Unconformity—a billion and a half years of the earth's history gone with the wind and rain.

For all 90,000,000 years of the Cambrian Period—first of seven periods of the Paleozoic Era—the sea occupied the Grand Canyon region. At first it was shallow, and islands of the Chuar and Unkar rocks rose above the waves. But these islands gradually were submerged, and up to eight hundred feet of mud and lime, which were to harden in time into the Bright Angel shale and Muav limestone, covered their rocks and the Tapeats sandstone. Life in this Cambrian Sea had come a long way since the algae (and perhaps jellyfish) that had inhabited the ocean in which the Bass limestone was laid down. Seaweeds swayed with the surf and the tides. Tiny animals with rounded shells and early relatives of the snail encrusted the offshore rocks or crawled about the ooze. And then there were the trilobites. Somewhat similar to the modern horseshoe crab, they attained a size in the Grand Canyon region of over three inches in length. This, combined with their numbers and their probably carnivorous appetites, must have made them the terrors

of the deep in their day. And their day was a long one. Their structure, though primitive, was sound enough for them to flourish for 200,000,000 years, and for much of that time they were, as Krutch puts it, the "kingpin of creation. . . . They lasted far longer than the dinosaurs were to last—to say nothing of man who, so far, has only a very brief history and may, for all we know, have only a very brief future. Trilobites had much better reason to suppose that the earth belonged to them than we have to assume that it belongs to us or that it was created primarily *for* us. If trilobites could have thought at all, they would probably have wondered, as foolish men still sometimes do, just which of their special needs this or that other living creature had been created to supply."

Complete as is the open book on the earth's history represented by the Grand Canyon, some chapters *are* missing. Two of the most important immediately follow the Cambrian chapter: the Ordovician, when fish first appeared in the seas, and the Silurian, when millipedes and scorpions became the first air-breathing animals. Perhaps sediments deposited during those 85,000,000 years were completely eroded away. More probably, geologists think, the whole region was raised above sea level, no sediments were deposited, and hence no rocks were formed. The next succeeding chapter, the Devonian or Age of Fish, is almost but not quite missing. Most of the formations of that period were washed away before it ended, but some pockets of limestone were left here and there in hollows previously eroded in the surface of the Muav. A slow-moving armored fish shared the Devonian waters with corals, brachiopods and gastropods, and its fossil plates and scales have turned up in these pockets of lavender Temple Butte limestone.

In the next period, the Mississippian, a deep, quiet sea invaded the region from the north. For 25,000,000 years skeletons of marine plants and animals—including brachiopods, corals and sea lilies—settled on the bottom. A deep layer of almost pure lime, including countless shells preserved in perfect detail, built up inch by inch, and eventually solidified into more than five hundred feet of blue-gray limestone, the formation known to us, for reasons already stated, as the Redwall. Then, once again, the sea withdrew.

The next two strata, laid down during the early Permian period, were alluvial deposits similar to the deltas at the mouth of the Colorado or Mississippi river in our time. Materials forming the red beds of the Supai Formation, one thousand feet thick, were brought down by rivers running from the northeast, and deposited in a wide, rather arid flood plain. Ferns and other low plants provided what shade there was. Amphibians or primitive reptiles left their tracks in the mud, some the size of small lizards, some heavier and more sluggish with footprints two or three inches across. Living conditions were much the same while the overlying three hundred feet of Hermit shale was being deposited, also by streams flowing from the northeast. But the forms of life were more varied. Thirty-five species of plants, principally ferns and small conifers, have been recovered from the Hermit shale. Tracks of worms, numerous footprints of amphibians and reptiles, and several insect wings, one of which was four inches in length, also have been found. Preserved in the shale are raindrop and hailstorm impressions, as well as the cracks that form in sun-dried mud, giving a picture of a region where showers and occasional violent torrents alternated with long, torrid periods of drought.

Gradually the climate became even more arid. The rivers dried up. And from the north, prevailing winds blew in vast quantities of sand, piling it up into huge dunes which eventually were to become the three-hundred-foot-thick, cross-bedded Coconino sandstone. No plant or animal fossils have been found in this stratum, but we know this Permian desert was not barren of life. Twenty-seven species of animals—small primitive amphibians or reptiles—left their tracks in its dunes.

At its greatest extent, the Coconino desert covered some thirty thousand square miles. But geologically speaking it was not of long duration. The Permian Period, which lasted 35,000,000 years, already had seen the deposition of the Supai and Hermit beds; and before it was over and the Mesozoic or "Middle Life" Era began, seas twice more covered the Grand Canyon region and twice more receded, leaving behind them six hundred feet or more of sandstones and massive limestones of the Toroweap and Kaibab formations. These seas came from far to the west, and their flora and fauna—shellfish of all kinds, corals, sponges, sea lilies—suggest that they were warm and shallow. Sharks too coursed the sunlit waters of the Kaibab sea, and their teeth have been found embedded in the limestone.

The Permian chapter ended some 200,000,000 years ago. And except for a minor appendix or two, it closes the Grand Canyon book on the region's sedimentary history. Not that further thousands of feet of rock were not laid down in the Mesozoic and Cenozoic Eras. But their stories must be read elsewhere—at Zion and Bryce Canyon national parks, for instance. In the Grand Canyon area they were all worn away, in what Dutton calls the Great Denudation. Of the Mesozoic—the Age of Dinosaurs—the only appreciable vestiges are two low mesas—Cedar Mountain near Desert View, and Red Butte south of Grand Canyon Airport. The Cenozoic is represented only by the volcanic formations near Toroweap Point in the Grand Canyon National Monument, the most recent of which are about thirty thousand years old.

The landscape at the end of the Great Denudation is described by John H. Maxson in *Grand Canyon: Origin and Scenery:* "The land stood near the level of the sea and the Colorado River was broad and sluggish as it flowed southwesterly in its wide and gentle valley. On a smaller scale it may have resembled portions of the courses of the Missouri and Mississippi rivers as it wound about and meandered over its flood plain. Oxbow lakes, cut-off and isolated meanders, flanked the stream. The water of the river was dark and loaded with red mud and silt. The surrounding country possessed little relief but here and there were residual low sandstone-capped buttes and mesas." Unlikely as it might appear from this description, the stage was set for the carving of the Grand Canyon.

Geologists argue as to just when this began, some claiming the process took between seven and nine million years, some insisting on a span of as many as 25,000,000 years. They also differ on many of the details—geology is an intuitive, not an exact, science. But the general story is clear enough. In another of those great periodic crustal movements, the whole plateau country gradually began to rise. This had a multiple effect on the Colorado and its tributaries. As the river's drop to the sea increased so did the speed of its current. As the river became swifter (and perhaps rose in volume, since precipitation tends to increase with greater elevation) it gained in capacity to carry along silt, sand grains, pebbles, and boulders—which acted as tools constantly gouging and cutting at the river bed as they moved. And with this new cutting power all the streams of the region began to deepen their gorges. The canyons were being born.

The regional uplift was particularly pronounced where the Grand Canyon lies today. The ground swelled up into a huge, gentle dome, 9,000 feet high at its peak on the North Rim's Kaibab Plateau. And this dome heaved up athwart the Colorado's channel. But though the river adjusted its course to certain dips in the strata and geological fault lines, it found the dome itself to be no obstacle. For the Colorado was always able to cut its gorge a little faster than the land was rising under it—a process that has been likened to a cake's being pressed upward against a stationary knife.

Every feature expresses that logic which we have come to find indispensable in the human architecture we most admire. For every feature there is a why and a wherefore. . . . Nowhere else are landscape and geology more intimately related, the one more clearly an expression of the other.

JOSEPH WOOD KRUTCH

CLYDE CHILDRESS: *Schist and pink granite, Granite Gorge*

CLYDE CHILDRESS: Detail of wall, Granite Gorge

There is no eye so trained, nor imagination so winged, that it can conceive from above the vastness, the mystery, the wonder of this subliminal world. And when one has sounded the depths, then one may sit on the rim, and "place" the giants around whose knees he has crawled, and "relate" depth and distance and the setting of the Titan stage.   CHARLES F. LUMMIS

In times of flood, the Colorado has transported as much as thirty-three million tons of rock past the Bright Angel gauging station in one day. Before Glen Canyon Dam partially plugged its flow, it used to move about 170,000,000 cubic yards of dirt per year—or more than enough to dig a Panama Canal every three years. With these tools, and millions of years in which to use them, it was able to carve its mile-deep gorge into the dome of the Kaibab, down through all the strata from the Kaibab limestone of the rims to the two billion year old mountain roots of the Inner Gorge.

Of course, if this were the whole story then the Grand Canyon ought to be a trench five or six thousand feet deep and only three hundred feet wide. Or we should have to believe that at one time in the past the river had been ten miles wide or more to be able to excavate the outer Canyon. The answer to this, naturally, is that while the river worked to deepen its channel other forces were ever widening the gorge. Frost action cracked the rocks. Plant roots wedged into the cracks, gradually prying them wider. Rain, wind, and the force of gravity worked the loosened materials down to the river, to be carried by it toward the sea. Imagine for a moment that these forces in collusion had widened the canyon by an inch, the width of one pebble, every year for twelve million years. The canyon would then be nearly two hundred miles wide! That it only averages ten miles from rim to rim through the Kaibab Plateau attests to the fact that this is and was a dry land, a "land of little rain."

"The finest workers in stone," Thoreau once wrote, "are not copper or steel tools, but the gentle touches of air and water working at their leisure with a liberal allowance of time." With such tools, and with ample time at its disposal, nature was able to carve the stupendous chasm of the Grand Canyon. But the Canyon is not only big. It is also a marvelously intricate composition of cliffs and benches, of cirques and points and lonely, majestic buttes. This complexity is a direct consequence of its fascinating geological history.

Different rocks weather in different ways. Hard rocks tend to form straight cliffs, weaker rocks to erode into slopes. Hence the stairstep profile of the outer Grand Canyon. The resistant limestones and sandstones—the Kaibab, Coconino, Redwall, Tapeats—form the Canyon's vertiginous cliffs. The softer layers—the sandy gradation member of the Toroweap, the shales of the Hermit, Supai and Bright Angel formations—erode into variously abrupt or gently curving benches. No master architect could have evolved a more harmonious plan.

Crustal stresses developed during the deposition of the Canyon's strata which at two different periods caused its rocks to fracture and slip along fault lines many miles long. As Dr. Maxson explains it, "the shattered rocks of fault zones are more easily further broken up and carried away by running water. Thus as the Colorado River persistently cut its channel to lower levels, tributary streams draining the canyon sides carved canyons in the shatter zones and extended their courses headward. Such tributaries, controlled in their growth by structure, are known as *subsequent* streams. These subsequent streams have eroded the network of the Outer Canyon. They account for the amphitheaters and cruciform valleys.

"The picturesque forms of the spurs between the subsequent streams, the spired promontories and stepped temples with their cliffs, curved deep embayments and re-entrants, are the impressive and memorable features of the Grand Canyon as a whole. To the imaginative they suggest buildings, castles and temples, ships and other creations of fantasy. On the spurs there is very little rainfall, so water flows only at rare intervals. Reduction proceeds through sapping at the cliff base and cliff retreat. The Redwall limestone, largest of all cliff-forming elements, suffers reduction of its cliff face by falling of gigantic spalls and enlarging rounded embayments or cirques. Here and there arched overhangs and shallow caves form." And as the Redwall retreats, so must all the formations above it. It is the controlling factor for the whole upper part of the Canyon.

One other peculiarity of the Grand Canyon—of that portion of it in the National Park, to be more exact—is immediately apparent to one standing on either rim. The North Rim is much farther from the river than the South Rim, and it is much more deeply and more fantastically etched. The reason for this is simple. In cutting through the dome, the Colorado passed to the south of the crest. As a result, the Coconino Plateau which forms the South Rim slopes away from the river, and whatever rain falls on it drains away to the south. Only such precipitation as falls below the rim reaches the river on that side; the creeks are small and intermittent, and have been able to cut back but little. The opposite is true on the north side of the Canyon. From the high point of the dome, the land slopes toward the river. Since the North Rim is at least 1,000 feet higher than the South it receives much greater precipitation, and this all drains into the river. Erosion has therefore proceeded much faster and farther; the side canyons are longer, the isolated buttes and mesas much more numerous and imposing, the side streams bigger and more constant in flow.

One of these streams is Bright Angel Creek. It was running strongly as we walked along it that afternoon to the oasis of Phantom Ranch. The Ranch, a cluster of rustic stone buildings set by the creek in a grove of cottonwoods, sycamores, and fruit trees, gave us a pleasant respite from the comparative rigors of the journey— hot showers, a huge roast beef dinner, and comfortable beds. A chorus of canyon tree toads was calling from the swimming pool outside our cabin as I tried to get to sleep. But for some reason—perhaps I missed the familiar roar of the river—sleep would not come. I found myself thinking back to that hike down the Kaibab Trail with the astronauts and U.S.G.S. instructors, to the lessons on geology I had learned that day. The vanished mountains. The vanished seas. The vanished trilobites.

By the inexorable forces of nature, the Grand Canyon too will vanish eventually. Some day in the far future the Canyon will again be a wide, gentle valley, with a sluggish Colorado River meandering through it. And then the sea may move in once again . . . the limey skeletons of its inhabitants will slowly pile up in the bottom ooze . . . a new layer of limestone will be formed . . . and gradually the earth will rise . . . and then I was asleep.

As arranged before the start of the trip, my wife left the party in the morning, clip-clopping off astride a mule on the five-hour climb up the Kaibab Trail to the South Rim. Two more men, photographers Clyde Childress and Carl Yost, joined our crew, thus increasing our number to ten. We pushed off into the stream under a cloudy sky at midmorning, having ascertained from the river gauger that the flow, which had been nearly 20,000 cubic feet per second for several days, was down to about 13,000. Except for the *Portola*, which made a number of circuits of a big eddy known as the Devil's Spittoon before it could get back into the current, we had a quick run down to Horn Creek Rapid, stopping just above it to look it over. It was rough. The rapid's total fall was only eight and a half feet—little enough when compared with Hance's twenty-seven and a half, Unkar's twenty-one, or Sockdologer's nineteen. But the shortness of Horn made its fall terribly abrupt, while the narrowness of the gorge at this point made the current awesomely swift. Horn was by no means impossible to run—Pat Reilly had run it in 1953 at the same stage of water; as a matter of fact, on typical trips in the past he and Martin Litton had run all the rapids with the exception of Lava Falls. But this trip was not typical. For one thing it was much earlier in the year than the usual one, its timing having been dictated by the release of water from Glen Canyon Dam. The weather was still cool—unseasonably

so, in fact, even for early May—and the water correspondingly frigid, which made us much more wary of risking an upset than we would have been in the heat of a normal summer traverse. Also the *Lucky Pierre* was an open boat, the second in history to have traversed the Grand Canyon, and more liable to swamp or to flip over than the others.* With these considerations in mind, Pat Reilly decided to portage the boats around the rapid on the left shore.

This was a slow, tedious job. Everything first had to be unloaded from the boats—camera gear, duffle bags, cans of food and all—and carried to the foot of the rapid. Then, after a lunch break, we picked up the boats one by one (they weighed from two hundred to four hundred pounds), carried them up a steep sand dune, along the foot of the cliff, and down an incline of unsteady boulders. It was a process of one, two, three, heave . . . take three or four stumbling steps, then let her down. After better than three hours' work we had the boats in the water and reloaded below Horn and were again on our way. An hour later we landed on the left above the mouth of Monument Creek, within sight and hearing of Granite Falls Rapid. We took a long look at the rapid, decided to line it in the morning, and made camp where we were.

It was a fine spot, with long graceful dunes and level stretches of sand bordered with tamarisk. The dark schist was intricately veined with the pink granite, which in some sections of the walls formed dominant patches of color. The overcast was breaking up at suppertime, and in the amber evening light the hues of the walls blended into a warm mauve. High above the upstream bend of the river, a conical knob on a spur of Dana Butte jutted into the skyline, and caught the rays of the setting sun. As the light dimmed around us the knob shone for some minutes like a beacon. Then it, too, went dark. Soon the stars were out, with Venus brilliant in the west.

Sitting by the campfire, listening to the drumming of Granite Falls Rapid, I thought for a minute of that big

*The reader should keep these special conditions in mind, lest my descriptions in this and other chapters discourage him from traversing the Grand Canyon himself. We had bad luck with the weather, and our trip was consequently far more strenuous than the usual one. Had we been able to start two weeks later than we did we would have had perfect weather all the way and I could have described a far more typical river journey. Hopefully, in future years the Bureau of Reclamation will release sufficient water during the summer months to allow the growing throng of river boating enthusiasts to enjoy that greatest of all river experiences—the Grand Canyon traverse. Unless, of course, they build Marble Gorge Dam, which would put an end to the river trips once and for all.

gray boulder by the shore. Pat Reilly, our geology expert, had pointed to it while we were examining the rapid, and quizzed me: "What kind of rock is that?" I looked at it carefully; the color, the texture, but especially the cherty nodules gave it away. "Kaibab limestone," I answered, which was right. That boulder, weighing a ton or more, had traveled all the way from the rim, the nearest projection of which, Mohave Point, was two linear miles and one vertical mile away. How long had it taken to reach its temporary resting place? Ten years? A century? A thousand years or more? How many rainstorms had been required to budge it an inch of the way? How many floods down Monument Creek to move it a few feet? No one could ever guess. But that block of Kaibab limestone was as convincing a demonstration as one could hope for of the forces of erosion at work in the Canyon, ever deepening it, ever widening it, ever toiling to move it and the canyon country to the sea.

Once again I thought, not without a pang of regret, that one day the Canyon would be no more. But of course I was losing my perspective of Time. A thousand years hence, a hundred thousand years hence, the Canyon would be much as it is today. And long before it would cease to deserve the name, "Grand Canyon," man himself might be just as dead as the trilobite. Let nature's forces have their play—the danger lay elsewhere, and it was far more immediate. It came from man and his technology and his frightening myopia. It came from those men who looked at the river and thought only of kilowatts; who looked at those Canyon walls, which the ages had built and the river had exposed, and thought of them only as convenient abutments for dams. If these men had their way—and they were perilously close to success—the Grand Canyon would be no smaller, but it would be diminished. It would have lost its soul—its wild, lonely, untamed soul.

The machine has divorced man from the world of nature to which he belongs, and in the process he has lost in large measure the powers of contemplation with which he was endowed. A prerequisite for the preservation of the canons of humanism is a reestablishment of organic roots with our natural environment and, related to it, the evolution of ways of life which encourage contemplation and the search for truth and knowledge. The flower and vegetable garden, green grass, the fireplace, the primeval forest with its wondrous assemblage of living things, the uninhabited hilltop where one can silently look at the stars and wonder—all of these things and many others are necessary for the fulfillment of man's psychological and spiritual needs. To be sure, they are of no "practical value" and are seemingly unrelated to man's pressing need for food and living space. But they are as necessary to the preservation of humanism as food is necessary to the preservation of human life. HARRISON BROWN

A poor society may ask only that its products be well engineered. But a richer one is certain to require that they have beauty as well.

In the earlier stages of industrialization the engineer is important. In the later stages he yields place to the artist. The practical man who holds that this is a lot of precious nonsense may, like the automobile makers, have to learn the truth the hard and expensive way. JOHN KENNETH GALBRAITH

That is all the National Parks are about. Use, but do no harm. WALLACE STEGNER

8. Bass Rapid

IT RAINED on and off during the night, and the day dawned raw and windy. We hung around the campfire or took short hikes up Monument Creek, hoping that the sun would break through before we must start to line Granite Falls Rapid. But the sun did not oblige, and at eleven o'clock we began the job of letting the boats down.

If I had any delusions that lining would be simple I was quickly disabused. In theory it sounded easy enough: let the current do the work, and just guide the boats by lines from the shore. In practice it was something else again. The "shore" was a jumble of car-sized boulders over and between which we clambered with our lines, some of the boulders slick and slippery, others covered with knife-edged flutings. More such rocks lay off-shore, between which we must thread the boats. Half the time the craft hung up on a submerged rock and must be manhandled off it. At one point, one of the boats "impinged": the current drove it against a rock, filled the boat and kept it pinned to the crag. While some of us belayed the craft to boulders on the bank, others waded out to the boat, the current sweeping fast and cold around our knees and waists. We heaved and pushed and pulled until at last the boat came free.

Tired, bruised, wet, and chilled, we finished the lining in mid-afternoon, then proceeded downstream. We did not get far. Twenty minutes after leaving Granite Falls we stopped on the left side above Hermit Rapid. We did not need to look it over long before concluding, for the same reasons that had led us to portage Horn and line Granite Falls, that we had better line Hermit too. A trifle discouraged, we decided to camp above the mouth of Hermit Creek. The creek was running clear and with a good-sized flow for a left bank stream. It was set about with much cactus, black-bush, catclaw, agave and some yucca, and two hundred yards or so back from the river the creek dropped in a series of beautiful little cascades, bordered by maidenhair fern and brilliant red flowers. Plants of the desert and of moist climates grew within a stone's throw of each other.

Another wet night paled into another cold, gray day, and this developed into an almost exact replica of its eve.

There was the morning mostly spent around the fire, in the forlorn hope that the day would warm up. There was the lining of Hermit, almost as rough a job as the lining of Granite Falls. There was the afternoon start down the river, with all of us already cold, wet, and tired. In this weather there was something forbidding about the Granite Gorge. As Dutton might have phrased it, the rocks, once merely dark, now appeared gloomy; the gorge, which had been only somber, now looked sinister; the river, which had been ominous, now seemed actively malevolent. The roar of a hidden rapid awaited us at almost every bend. Boucher, Crystal, Tuna, Agate, Sapphire, Turquoise succeeded each other, each named for the side canyon that reached the river at that point. Such names as Bear, Tiger, Dragon—and something particularly ferocious-sounding for Sapphire—would have been more suitable for the rapids themselves. The river drenched us in the rough stretches; the sky dripped on us in between. We stopped for a short while and lit a big driftwood bonfire by which we thawed out a bit. But the relief was short-lived, and we were a bedraggled-looking crew when we landed in late afternoon on the left shore, at the mouth of Ruby Canyon.

The place had something of the quality of a Japanese brush-and-ink drawing. It was a study in black and white: the jet black of the schist, polished at the water's edge to an almost obsidian finish; the white of the fine-grained sand that piled into swelling dunes in the opening of the side canyon. The schist itself was veined with pegmatite, and a pure white dike of the mineral snaked down the canyon wall to our kitchen spot.

We turned in before nightfall under glowering skies, and prepared as best we could for another night of rain. We were not disappointed. In the morning the temperature was a few degrees above freezing, and squalls of rain and hail whipped us as we prepared for the day. Obviously something was drastically wrong with the weather —for was this not the month of May in sunny Arizona? Our veterans, Pat and Susie Reilly and Martin Litton, cheerfully described the hot, bright days they always had experienced on other boat trips through the Canyon. But this did little to warm us up, or to make us look forward to the wettings that awaited us. We had some big water ahead of us: Ruby, Serpentine, Bass. "We'll run Bass ackwards," offered Joe Hall. Indeed the cheer was somber, and the jests were ghastly.

The river at this point flowed north northwest, in the direction of Powell Plateau, a large semi-detached projection of the North Rim. Through the rain and low-slung clouds the Plateau could be seen indistinctly, framed in the jagged V of the Inner Gorge's walls. Suddenly there came a fleeting moment of great beauty. The rain stopped, the clouds over the Plateau lifted and parted, and its cliffs and slopes glowed in the sun. From our vantage point it was rather like sitting in a darkened theater, looking at a brightly lit stage. There was a sparkle of fresh snow, from the rim of the Plateau down to the top of the Redwall. The rose hue of the Redwall, the pale green of the Tonto Platform below it, were a cheerful splash of color between the white above and the black of the Inner Gorge. Then, as suddenly as they had parted, the clouds closed in again, Powell Plateau vanished behind a shroud, and rain began to fall around us.

It was probably snowing up there on the rim, and I remembered one afternoon three months earlier when I had stood on the South Rim, braced against the whistling wind, with snowflakes hissing all about me. Swirling gray clouds of snow filled the void at my feet, blotting out my view of the Canyon. But once in a while the curtains would half part, and I would get a glimpse, a fleeting hint, of the mysteries of the Canyon's depths.

The next morning I had driven out to Desert View, my tires crunching over the snow, in time to see the sun rise. Broken clouds to the east shone scarlet from the fat red globe of the sun, and the Painted Desert glowed with iridescent color, backed by the dark line of the Echo Cliffs at the horizon and with the canyon of the Little Colorado snaking blackly through the middle ground. Snow mantled the Grand Canyon below me almost to the Inner Gorge, but the reds of its cliffs and buttes were lit up with the rising sun. To the west, dark storm clouds overhung the Canyon, and cottony patches of fog filled some of its recesses. The scene was almost garish.

On some clear winter days, fog will fill the Canyon from rim to rim like a gigantic snow field—it was on such days that Hance would claim he had snowshoed across the chasm. But most winter days at the South Rim are clear and mild, with temperatures in the midforties and fifties and dropping below freezing only at night. The transition from winter to summer is abrupt. The flowers bloom forth, but spring is apt to be an alternation of warm, summery days and of late snow flurries—

as we were learning to our occasional consternation on our river journey. Then suddenly it is summer, with daytime temperatures in the mid-eighties. June is a dry month, but thunderstorms are frequent in July and August, and they are one of the most awesome phenomena in the Canyon.

Autumn, unlike spring, is lingering on the South Rim, and grades imperceptibly into the clear, crisp days of winter. The character of the seasons is somewhat different on the North Rim. Since it averages 1,000 feet higher than the South, its climate is more rigorous. Two hundred inches or more of snow may fall on the Kaibab Plateau between October and May, and the road into the National Park is blocked during winter. But by early May, the cold blasts sweeping down through Kaibab National Forest from the north will have given way to gentler winds blowing across the Canyon from the deserts to the south. On the southern extremities of the North Rim, on Point Sublime or Cape Royal, for instance, warm updrafts from the inner Canyon have brought spring flowers to bloom; cactus, agave, and the fragrant cliffrose have put out brilliant blossoms, and the noon air is like midsummer's. Back of the rim, snow banks linger at the forest's edge, but the deer and other wildlife have begun to return from winter quarters, and the long, open, level "parks" that are such a distinctive feature of the Kaibab Plateau are aglow with spring flowers.

Summer brings to bloom countless field and mountain flowers—lupine, gilia, iris, Queen-Anne's-lace, forget-me-not, scarlet bugler—and the fragrance of locust is heady along the road to Cape Royal. But it is perhaps in autumn that the North Rim achieves its greatest splendor. The aspen, which in summer form a curtain of green and silver against the darker tones of spruce and fir, gradually turn lemon yellow. From day to day the color deepens, until, in early October, the hillsides are resplendent with a mantle of gold.

Stupendous as the Grand Canyon is in its physical dimensions, climatically it assumes the proportions of a continent. For at the Canyon, or within a short distance of it, are represented all the climates and associated life zones of the North American continent with the sole exception of the tropics. Just forty miles southeast of the Canyon as the raven flies, the San Francisco Mountains culminate in Humphreys Peak, an extinct volcano 12,680 feet high. Above timberline on this majestic cone are found forty-nine species of plants, many of which are widely distributed in Arctic regions of North America and Eurasia, as well as on high mountain ranges such as the Sierra Nevada, Rocky Mountains, Alps and Himalayas. Presumably these plants migrated south during the last glacial period, then were forced upward as the glaciers retreated and temperatures became warmer.

At the very top of the Kaibab Plateau, near 9,000 feet altitude, are found a few "indicator plants" of the Hudsonian zone—alpine fir and Englemann spruce. A little lower on the Kaibab the trees are those typical of the Canadian zone. This is the beautiful virgin forest of Douglas fir, of the symmetrical Christmas-tree white fir and blue spruce, and of the white-barked aspen, often called quaking aspen because the slightest breeze sets its leaves to shivering and shimmering.

Still lower, below 7,500 feet, lies the Transition zone, characterized in the Grand Canyon region by the ponderosa pine. This beautiful, stately tree, with its orange-and-black bark, occupies only a narrow strip back of the South Rim. But it constitutes much of the timber in the Kaibab forest and is heavily logged to the north of the National Park. It grows in association with the Gamble's oak, flowering locusts, and such perennials as scarlet bugler, canyon lupine and blue penstemon.

The rims themselves belong to the Lower Sonoran zone, where the dominant flora is the pygmy forest of juniper and pinyon pine. Other plants include the small-leaved mountain mahogany, the cliff-rose, the manzanita, filaree, goldenrod, sego lily and Solomon's seal. Gradually, as one descends into the inner Canyon, the climate grows hotter and drier, and one enters the Lower Sonoran zone. It is perfectly possible in the summer to start the day high up on Humphreys Peak, and end it at Phantom Ranch. The distance traveled will have been fifty-odd miles in a straight line. But the journey is equivalent in climatic and vegetational changes to a four thousand mile trip from Point Barrow, Alaska, to Guaymas, Mexico. The inner Canyon is a desert region: low annual precipitation, mild winters, and torrid summers during which the daytime temperature can reach 120°. Along the immediate edge of the river grow such moisture-loving plants as willows and tamarisks—the latter not a native plant at all but one originally imported from the Near East to Southern California whence it has gradually made its way up the Colorado. But a few yards, or even feet, back from the river the plants are the heat-and-drought resistant forms of the desert—catclaw and mesquite, burro brush and sagebrush, barrel, hedgehog and prickly pear cacti, yucca and agave. And the perennials have the brilliant coloring characteristic of desert wildflowers: blue larkspur, scarlet mallow, and the gaudy crimson of Indian paintbrush.

Standing in the cold rain on the beach by Ruby Rapid, I found it difficult to accept that we were in a desert environment. And yet the evidence was there. If it was raining on our camp, which was at an altitude of about 2,200 feet, it was snowing on the rim of the Powell Plateau, 7,500 feet high. And those flowering agave growing in interstices of the Canyon walls' rocks were assurance that our present discomfort was only transitory. We took off finally about 10:30, ran Ruby Rapid without difficulty despite the big water in it, and a half hour later landed at the head of Serpentine Rapid. It was rough—so rough, in fact, that it was decided that the boatmen would run it solo and pick up their passengers down below. Pat Reilly made it through in a beautiful, dancing run. But Bill Jones started too far out; he quickly was drawn into the worst of the rapid, stayed upright through the first monster wave but took the next one on his quarter and was flipped like a pancake. I saw Jones' head bob up alongside the boat's red hull as both were swept downstream, with Reilly, who had picked up his own passengers, in pursuit. Martin Litton came through next in a well-executed run, took us all aboard, and we sped down the river after the others. We found them on the left shore, a half mile below the rapid, the *Lucky* (?) *Pierre* already righted and bailed out.

We boarded our respective boats and continued downstream for a little more than a mile to the head of Bass Rapid, where we landed for camp on the right. Six avocets in mating plumage with bright orange topknots took off from the shore as we approached, flew low over the water for some distance upstream, then turned around and came right back, landing a few yards away from the boats.

The Inner Gorge was slumped at this point, the granite forming a low bluff above our wide, rocky beach. We climbed the bluff easily, and found ourselves on a wide bench sloping down from the cliff of the Tapeats sandstone—it was on this bench that Stanton had planned to locate his train switching yard. Downriver to the northwest, the mass of Powell Plateau loomed over our heads, its horizontal strata delineated as clearly as they would be on a geological sketch. We noticed that the snow had melted during the day from below the rim; and indeed the temperature was rising and the sun breaking through the clouds as we walked along the bench. After the cold of the past four days and this day's mishap that sun was the most beautiful sight in the Canyon.

Wild burro hoofprints, large and small, were numerous along the bench, and we followed a well-worn burro trail. We found one place which the animals used for a

JOSEPH G. HALL: *Bassarisk and insect tracks, Salt Creek Canyon*

JOSEPH G. HALL: *Deer and fawn at Greenland Lake, on the Kaibab*

JOSEPH G. HALL: *Black-chinned hummingbird in catclaw, President Harding Rapid*

JOSEPH G. HALL: *Bobcat drinking, Harvey Spring*

. . . Exploiters who followed the explorers have been busy both at home and abroad rooting up, exterminating or merely pushing to the wall species after species in order to make room for themselves and for "useful" products. The variety of nature grows less and less. The monotony of the chain store begins to dominate more and more completely. One must go farther and farther to find a window in which anything not found elsewhere is to be seen.

More than a hundred species and subspecies of mammals are known to have disappeared from the face of the earth since the beginning of the Christian era. Along with them have gone perhaps as many birds and an unknown number of humbler creatures. How many plants have suffered extinction has not, so far as I am aware, been even guessed at. JOSEPH WOOD KRUTCH

JOSEPH G. HALL: Kaibab squirrel

PHILIP HYDE: Collared lizard

JOSEPH G. HALL: Bighorn sheep near Elves' chasm

JOSEPH G. HALL: Canyon tree toad, Phantom Canyon

The desert, being an unwanted place, might well be the last stand of life against unlife. For in the rich and moist and wanted areas of the world, life pyramids against itself and in its confusion has finally allied itself with the enemy non-life. And what the scorching, searing, freezing, poisoning weapons of non-life have failed to do may be accomplished to the end of its destruction and extinction by the tactics of survival gone sour. If the most versatile of living forms, the human, now fights for survival as it always has, it can eliminate not only itself but all other life. And if that should transpire, unwanted places like the desert might be the harsh mother of repopulation. . . . The desert has mothered magic things before this.   JOHN STEINBECK dust bath, and our expectations of seeing one rose. The glorious blooms of beavertail and hedgehog cacti opened to the sun, and a yellow composite grew profusely in the rocky soil. Just off the trail I noticed a ring of stones, perhaps ten or twelve feet in diameter, which quite possibly had once been the foundation of an aboriginal pithouse. We discovered no shards, but Phil Hyde picked up an arrowhead nearby—and lying almost next to it a rusted Winchester rifle cartridge.

Returning along the trail to the camp, we were walking up a rise when over its crest a burro came trotting toward us. He stopped short, and we did also. We eyed each other for a minute, then he gave a snort, his sides heaved and he let out a loud bray. He stepped off the path, trotted a short distance up the slope to our left, and stopped again to look us over. He was a fine-looking jack, well-muscled and handsomely marked, with a white nose, white rings around his eyes, white on his belly and inside his legs, and otherwise a dark gray. He seemed more curious about us than afraid, and perhaps a little vexed also, as he had a right to be.

Other than a few half-tame deer at Phantom Ranch, this was the first large mammal we had seen during the trip. We apparently had just missed meeting a coyote at our first campsite below the Little Colorado, and I had often heard *Canis latrans* bark and howl at night on the South Rim. One night in particular, when I was camped alone among the ponderosas just south of the Park, I had been awakened about one in the morning by what sounded like a chorus of banshees. After a confused second or two I realized the noise was coming from a pair of coyotes. They couldn't have been more than a few yards away—between the staccato barks and high-pitched howls I could hear low *grrrrufffs*, like those of a dog uncertain whether or not to bark. But though the moon was full and snow covered the ground, and there was no underbrush to obscure my view between the dark boles of the trees, I could not see the little wolves. But I had no doubt that they could see me, and that their loud commentary was directed at me. I listened to them for about five minutes, then metamorphosed into a *Homo latrans*. I barked back at them, imitating their rhythm and pitch as well as I could. This seemed greatly to amuse them, for it set them off into a paroxysm of barking and howling, in which I joined at appropriate intervals. This went on for perhaps ten minutes; then they fell silent, after a few final *grrrrufffs*, and must have stolen away through the forest. For a few moments, my world had intersected with the world of these wild creatures, and we had communicated with each other.

I had often sat on the rim of the Canyon, feeding peanuts to the pretty, friendly Gila chipmunks and to the bright blue pinyon jays, or admiring the flight of the ravens. Sometimes a raven would take off from a ledge below the rim, fly out over the void, fold its wings and drop hundreds of feet like a stone, open its wings again and level off with three croaking caws, an expression of its pure enjoyment of the gift of flight. But while there was life around me on the rim, it seemed difficult to believe that anything lived in those rocky depths. They appeared as dead as the craters of the moon. And yet many animals do live in the Canyon, and find its harsh wilderness very much to their liking.

The life zones classification applies to animals as well as to plants, although some animals, like the deer, coyote, bobcat, or mountain lion, can range freely from zone to zone. The fauna of the Canyon bottom is Lower Sonoran, made up of animals especially adapted to desert conditions. Except for birds, reptiles are the most frequently seen animals of the inner Canyon: the small earless lizards, fast-moving leopard lizards, the large, plant-eating chuckwalla, the spectacular collared lizard—the male of which is often a vivid green and the female bright orange, both with a conspicuous white band around the neck—the handsomely banded black and white Boyle's king snake. There is also a rare form of rattlesnake, the Grand Canyon rattler, whose pink color blends in with the background.

Mammals of the Lower Canyon include the antelope ground squirrel, which scurries from shrub to shrub with white tail held aloft like a flag; the desert wood rat, pocket mice, the kangaroo rat, which hops along on its hind feet and never needs a drink of water, the ringtailed cat, the little spotted skunk, and the bighorn sheep.

The wildlife of the Upper Sonoran zone is quite different. Reptiles are fewer—they include the swift and *Uta* lizards, the "horned toad," which is really a lizard, and the large but amiable gopher snake. Typical mammals are the prairie dog, cottontail rabbit, grasshopper mouse, gray fox, and various white-footed mice and wood rats. Reptiles are still fewer in the next higher, or Transition, zone. Mammals include the mantled ground squirrels, bushy-tailed wood rats, several varieties of pocket gophers, the porcupine, and the Arizona skunk. But the most typical and most unusual animals of the ponderosa or yellow pine belts are the tassel-eared squirrels. And they illustrate an interesting peculiarity of the Grand Canyon.

The Abert's of the South Rim and the Kaibab of the

North are large, beautiful squirrels, twenty inches long, with bushy nine-inch tails, and with tassels on their ears in winter—the only squirrels in the United States with such decorations. Both kinds are entirely dependent on the ponderosas for their food, eating the seeds when they are plentiful and otherwise feeding on the phloem, the sweet inner bark, of the branch tips. But despite their similarity in size, shape, and habits, the Abert's and Kaibab are different animals.

The Abert's squirrel in summer is brown on its back, gray on the sides, and pure white underneath. Its bushy tail is silver below and gray above. Its winter coloring is even more beautiful, with a narrow black band between the gray sides and white underparts. The Kaibab, on the other hand, is a rich chestnut brown on upper head and back. Its sides are a deep gray and its underparts are gray to black. And its great plumed tail is either all silver-white or white with a barely discernible light gray edging on the upper surface.

These differences, however, are so superficial that biologists agree that both squirrels are of common ancestry. Probably at the time of the last ice age the climate in the Canyon was cool and wet enough to allow ponderosas to grow right down to the river, and the squirrels could communicate from side to side. But with the subsequent warming of the weather the trees retreated upward, and the squirrels with them. Interbreeding between North and South Rim squirrels no longer was possible—the Canyon, and especially the desert climate of its interior, proved an impassable barrier. And gradually the squirrels on opposite sides of the gorge developed into two different strains. As Dr. McKee puts it, "We appear to have in the tassel-eared squirrels a fine example of evolution in its first stages, not well-defined in its trends and not yet in operation for a very long period, but having definite opportunities to develop well-isolated forms along independent lines."

Other small animals are unable to cross the physical and climatic barrier of the Canyon, and are represented by different species on opposite sides. For instance, the Utah cliff chipmunk, Colorado pocket gopher, yellow-haired porcupine, Utah gopher snake of the North Rim have as their counterparts on the South Rim the Gila chipmunk, fulvous pocket gopher, Arizona porcupine, and Arizona gopher snake.

The Abert's squirrel ranges far from the South Rim into portions of Colorado, Utah, New Mexico, and Mexico. But the Kaibab squirrel is absolutely confined to a small area, thirty by seventy miles, on the North Rim. And even there it is extremely scarce: only rarely may one see the white flash of its tail in the dark of the forest. As a result of its beauty, rarity, and scientific interest, the Kaibab was protected from hunting from 1906 until 1964, when suddenly the Arizona Game and Fish Department announced its intention to permit shooting of the squirrels during a one-week wild turkey hunt in the fall. The squirrels in the National Park, of course, would be safe. But most of the ponderosa pine acreage is in the National Forest north of the Park, and the major proportion of the Kaibab squirrel population is there, with the principal concentration around Jacob Lake.

National Park Service and Forest Service protests were unheeded, and apparently the survival of these beautiful animals was to be sacrificed to the whims of trophy-hunters. Irston R. Barnes, Chairman of the Audubon Naturalist Society, wrote that "The Kaibab squirrel cannot, of course, be eliminated by one season's hunting but its population can be so seriously reduced that recovery becomes impossible." And the *Washington Post* was moved to say in an editorial: "Since the Kaibabs are already extremely scarce, Arizona hunters can now slaughter the rest, or most of them. It is a commentary on the quality of humankind that men derive pleasure from killing anything so charming and harmless as a Kaibab squirrel, especially since the dead animal is not needed for its food or pelt. So the Kaibab squirrel will follow the Carolina parakeet, the passenger pigeon, and presently the whooping crane into oblivion in order that a few Arizonans may have the pleasure of shooting them. We hope that for every Kaibab squirrel shot, a score of tourists will give Arizona a wide berth. Perhaps then the Arizona Game and Fish Commission will regret the destruction of one more natural asset."

Such protests, and a deluge of mail and telegrams to Arizona Governor Paul Fannin, apparently unnerved the Game and Fish people for they finally canceled the turkey hunt and thus, indirectly, the squirrel shoot. But they gave no assurance that the threat would not be renewed another year.

Aside from moral and aesthetic considerations, what may be the ecological effect on the Kaibab Forest of the extinction of the squirrels? Not enough is known of their ecology to make a prediction. But once already, man's interference with the balance of nature on the Kaibab has proved disastrous. Before 1905, about 4,000 Rocky Mountain mule deer had lived in the Kaibab Forest. Their population was kept stable by the mountain lions or cougars which were numerous in the area. But then "Uncle Jim" Owen moved into the region with his pack of trained hunting dogs and went to war on the cougar. In twenty years he succeeded in killing at least six hundred. The deer, delivered of their surest control, multiplied fast, until by 1924 they numbered about 100,000. Then it was realized that the deer were badly over-browsing the forest, and that unless something was done soon the forest would be destroyed and the deer would die of starvation.

Attempts to drive and corral the deer in order to export them from the area proved futile, so the decision was made to permit controlled deer hunts. Such hunts (two or three a year) have been held ever since, the deer herd has been reduced to more normal proportions, and the vegetation has come back.

At the same time, a halt was called to the extermination of the mountain lion. But his numbers were so reduced that he has not recovered. It is estimated that at present there may be eight or ten cougars in Grand Canyon National Park. And even they are not safe. They will not be molested so long as they remain within the Park. But the cougar is a wide-ranging animal, and predator control has been resumed in the area. Control posts have been set up within three miles of the Park boundary, and it seems more than likely that in time they will dispose of the last of the Grand Canyon's mountain lions.

Predator control in the Western states—the use of steel traps and poison, the paying of bounties for coyotes, bobcats and mountain lions—has been characterized by the Secretary of the Interior's Advisory Board of Wildlife Management as "futile and wasteful" and its practice described as "considerably in excess of the amount that can be justified in terms of total public interest." In one California Forest Service region, for example, sheep losses in 1962 were reported at $3,500, while predator control cost around $90,000. University of California zoölogist A. Starker Leopold, chairman of the board of experts, commented that "The aesthetic value of coyotes greatly exceeds any potential damage they might cause."

This attitude is reminiscent of Thoreau. "I spend a considerable portion of my time," he wrote, "observing the habits of the wild animals, my brute neighbors. But when I consider that the nobler animals have been exterminated here—the cougar, panther, lynx, wolverine, bear, moose, deer, the beaver, the turkey, etc., etc.,—I cannot but feel as if I lived in a tamed and, as it were, emasculated country. Would not the motions of these larger and wilder animals have been more significant still? Is it not a maimed and imperfect nature that I am conversant with? As if I were to study a tribe of Indians that had lost all its warriors. . . . Primitive Nature is most interesting to me. I take infinite pains to know all the phenomena of spring, for instance, thinking that I have here the entire poem, and then, to my chagrin, I hear that it is but an imperfect copy that I possess and have read, that my ancestors have torn out many of the first leaves and grandest passages, and mutilated it in many places. I should not like to think that some demigod had come before me and picked out some of the best of the stars. I wish to know an entire heaven and an entire earth."

9. Kanab Creek

ENCOURAGED BY our meeting with the burro, we set off the next morning with hopes of seeing other large wildlife. To me, the mountain lion represented the soul of the wild, but I realized that sighting one of the big cats would be a stroke of the greatest luck. There was a better chance that we might spot some bighorns, and between rapids—Bass, Shinumo, Hakatai, Waltenburg—we kept a sharp lookout for them.

Beyond Waltenburg the river described a deep U around Marcos Terrace and Explorers Monument, which jutted south from Powell Plateau. The schist of the inner walls was increasingly low, and tended more and more to be buried under a talus slope topped by the thin-layered brown wall of Tapeats sandstone. We were rounding the bottom of the U when we saw the sheep on the talus to our right. Two rams with great, heavy, curling horns stood motionless as we approached. Then, with a few light bounds from boulder to boulder they climbed a little higher up the slope and stopped, eyeing us from their vantage point. They stood side by side, their heads held high, and like the burro showed no real alarm at our presence. They did not look much like domestic sheep: they were much larger, and their grayish coats instead of being woolly were sleek and smooth like the coats of deer. Nor did they display that vacuous expression usually associated with ovines. They had an alert, self-possessed, and haughty look about them which stamped them as true citizens of the wilderness.

Three hundred yards farther we landed on the left at the mouth of Royal Arch Creek to fill our water containers. A large tamarisk was in bloom, and its fragrance was sharp in the sun-warmed air. A pair of spotted sandpipers acted very perturbed, as if they had a nest in the vicinity. I followed the creek back from the river, and found that past floods had blocked its narrow canyon with room-sized boulders, which dammed the little stream into a series of exquisite falls and pools. Pollywogs darted in and out of the algae that gave a green tinge to the pools; the damp rocks were festooned with maidenhair fern, and scarlet monkeyflower bloomed at the water's edge. Farthest from the river were the highest fall and deepest pool—so deep that one could safely dive into it from the ledges above. The huge boulders lodged in the canyon's narrow slot formed a child's paradise of windows and tunnels and caves; Elves' Chasm, this oasis was called, and in its austere and august Canyon setting it certainly had a fairyland quality.

A little more than a mile below Elves' Chasm the Upper Granite Gorge came to an end, and the river ran on between cliffs of Tapeats sandstone. The brown sandstone formed undulating overhangs and had been washed a creamy color to the high water mark of the river. Soon the gorge turned west again and we entered Conquistador Aisle, a glorious straight section about three miles long, with the Canyon's red and buff upper cliffs continuously in view. At its end the river swung again to the right and headed northeastward between the looming bulks of Great Thumb Mesa and Powell Plateau. We plunged through Forster Rapid, Fossil Rapid—a long S-shaped stretch of rough water at the mouth of Fossil Bay—and ran into the schist and granite once more.

The Middle Granite Gorge was different in character from the Upper, far less brooding and confining. Its walls were lower and less abrupt, and even at river level we had frequent spectacular views of the Great Thumb on the left and Powell Plateau and Steamboat Mountain to the right. The bright sun brought into relief the marvelous details of the Redwall with its caves and alcoves and arching overhangs. We stopped at one point to take a close look at the schist. Here it was blacker than any rock I had ever seen, black and shiny as anthracite coal, and sculptured by the water into flutings and potholes that seemed to have a fluid movement of their own. The rock had absorbed the heat of the sun, and wet from our passage through the rapids we lay flat on its smooth surface like big lizards and let the delicious warmth seep into our bones.

Our stop was brief, and soon we were back in the boats, flushing through Hundred and Twenty-eight Mile Rapid, past Specter Chasm, through Specter Rapid, by the 2,000 foot elevation point, and, after an examination, into Bedrock Rapid. This one was rather harrowing: a big islet of bedrock squatted in midstream; the surge of the current bore straight down upon it, and split against its mass into two channels. The left channel was

CLYDE CHILDRESS: Elves' Chasm, Mile 116.5

I climb so high that the men and boats are lost in the black depths below and the dashing river is a rippling brook, and still there is more canyon above than below. All about me are interesting geologic records. The book is open and I can read as I run. All about me are grand views, too, for the clouds are playing again in the gorges. . . .

I go up a little stream to the north, wading it all the way, sometimes having to plunge in to my neck, in other places being compelled to swim across little basins that have been excavated at the foot of the falls. Along its course are many cascades and springs, gushing out from the rocks on either side.

JOHN WESLEY POWELL

a nightmare of rocks and holes and haystacks—Heaven help any boat that got drawn into that! One after the other we slid down the tongue; larger and larger and closer and closer loomed the great rock, while the boatmen pulled to the right as hard as they could. But the current was stronger than they . . . it hurled us irresistibly towards the boulder island . . . we were going to hit . . . *look out!* But at the last critical moment we slid by to the right, riding high onto the buffer wave which washed against the side of the islet. A few more moments of tossing and plunging and we were through. And twenty minutes later we put in to the right shore at the head of Dubendorff Rapid and made camp for the night. It had been a good day; the weather had been sunny and warm, the rapids had been fun, and we had covered almost twenty-four miles, our best day's mileage of the trip to date.

The boatmen ran solo in the morning through Dubendorff, and the big rapid proved a match for them. Martin Litton was spun around by one wave, and ended up "Major Powelling" the rest of the way—i.e., rowing with his back downstream. Water was dripping from his hat and his face was creased in a rueful smile when he hit the rocky beach below to pick up his passengers. The river presently began to curve toward the west, and two miles below Dubendorff we passed the mouth of Tapeats Creek, which flowed crystal clear from the right. We had hoped to hike up the creek to its twin sources at Thunder and Tapeats Springs, where the water gushes out from the Redwall in a series of spectacular falls lined with lush verdure, but our slow progress between Bright Angel Creek and Bass Rapid had put us behind schedule and we had to move on.

A tenth of a mile below Tapeats Creek we reached the point where the National Park's northern boundary came down to the river. For the next eleven miles the right bank would be National Forest land. And this meant, among other things, that one of the loveliest sights in Grand Canyon, Deer Creek Falls, was excluded from the Park where by all criteria—those of logic and topography as well as aesthetics—it belonged. We landed at the falls just before noon, in a constricted portion of the gorge known as Granite Narrows. From a narrow cleft in the Tapeats sandstone about 125 feet above our heads Deer Creek plunged in an uninterrupted fall, slender, white, and lacy like a bridal veil. Maidenhair fern and scarlet monkeyflower draped the walls on either side of the fall; the water landed in a deep blue pool rimmed with boulders, and the wind caused by the fall watered a thick growth among the boulders.

We scaled the Inner Gorge to the left of the falls, and followed a ledge into Deer Creek's miniature canyon. The creek had cut a sinuous course through the Tapeats, and the gorge offered a striking contrast between erosion by wind and rain and erosion by running water. The fifty feet or so of the canyon above our heads had been exposed to the elements longest; the weather had cut away at the walls, and blocks of the thin-bedded sandstone had broken off, leaving angular recesses and projections. Below our feet snaked the creek's inner trench, barely twelve feet wide. Here the creek's action had been more recent; the sides were smooth and rounded and beautifully scalloped. At first, as I proceeded back along the ledge, I could only hear the creek's thunder from deep inside its trench. Gradually, as the trench grew more shallow the sound came closer, and after about two hundred yards I reached the upper falls. The creek tumbled in a series of low cascades separated by level stretches where the gravel mosaic of the stream bed showed clearly through the crystal water. Water ouzels flew up and down the creek and frequently disappeared behind a fall, where presumably they had nests. At the lip of the first fall stood a magnificent cottonwood, four feet in diameter. And around the final bend we issued from the gorge into a valley on the Tonto Platform, and discovered a whole grove of cottonwoods bordering the course of the creek. In this land of few large trees it was like running into an oasis of palms in the desert, and the place was aptly called Surprise Valley. Not that the Tonto, stretching up to the foot of the majestic Redwall, was barren—far from it. It was in full spring bloom, bright with cactus flowers, the apricot blossoms of desert mallow, lavender mariposa lilies with purple and yellow centers like a pansy's, yellow daisies and blue phacelia.

We retraced our steps to the boats and pushed out into the current. The Middle Granite Gorge ended immediately below Deer Creek, and soon we found ourselves in a section of the Canyon which was very much like the Marble Gorge. Its sides glowed with the warm red tones of the Redwall and Muav limestones, which reared in high, straight cliffs above the river-side talus slopes. The warmth of the day matched the warmth of the colors, and we ran Hundred and Thirty-eight Mile Rapid, Fishtail Rapid—and two or three riffles which kicked up a splash at this low stage of water—with unmitigated enjoyment of the bouncing rides. We put in to the left for the night a few hundred yards upstream from Kanab Creek, on a steep sandy shelf atop a Muav limestone ledge. A dry creek bed bordered with catclaw

What one finds . . . will be what one takes the trouble to look for—the brilliant little flower springing improbably out of the bare, packed sand, the lizard scuttling with incredible speed from cactus clump to spiny bush, the sudden flash of a bright-colored bird. This dry world, all of which seems so strange to you, is normal to them. It is their paradise, their universe as-it-ought-to-be. . . .   JOSEPH WOOD KRUTCH

PHILIP HYDE: Detail, dune at Dubendorff Rap

ran down from an alcove in the Redwall shaped like the apse of a gigantic church. A great cottonwood trunk, three feet in diameter, was balanced on a limestone boulder twenty feet above the river, testimony to the power of the Colorado in flood. Alas, the chances were slim that the river would again roar by here at flows of 100,000 or 200,000 cubic feet per second—at least not until Lake Powell was silted in leaving Glen Canyon Dam standing as a monument to man's shortsightedness. Every ounce of water not absolutely necessary to meet power and irrigation commitments from Hoover Dam down would be trapped behind Glen Canyon Dam so *its* generators could produce power. Even at the 10,000 to 20,000 cfs which we had enjoyed on our trip the Colorado could put on a brave show, but we knew that it was a command performance which men could turn on and off at will by manipulating the gates of Glen Canyon Dam. The Colorado could still be wild but the beast was, so to speak, behind bars.

Nevertheless, the mud in the river spoke of tributaries not yet barred. The Bureau of Reclamation liked to boast that with the building of Glen Canyon Dam they had transformed the Colorado into a clear-running stream. We had found on our trip that this "miracle of clear water" was a myth. Even if every tributary creek could be dammed, and every side canyon blocked from Glen Canyon Dam down, the run-off from storms would still find its way to the river, laden with the products of erosion. One thing, however, Glen Canyon Dam would in time accomplish. It takes flows of 100,000 cubic feet per second for the river to move the grosser detritus—the coarse gravel, rocks and boulders—brought down by the tributaries. Such flows used to occur regularly in the spring floods. By preventing these flows the dam will cause this detritus to pile up at the mouth of the side canyons. And this will result, eventually, in ponding the river behind a series of boulder dams which themselves will form really impassable rapids.

House finches, canyon wrens, kingbirds, and yellow warblers were singing in the morning as we awoke early beneath a cloudless sky. Immediately after breakfast we set off, crossing to the north bank and drifting down along it to the mouth of Kanab Creek, where we landed. The creek in flood had deposited an extensive silt flat through which it had cut an outlet, and behind the flat a large, still lagoon mirrored the canyon walls. To the left, or west, of the lagoon the wind had piled up streamlined sand dunes on the edge of which grew a line of tamarisks with roots exposed, seeming to stand on stilts. I hiked back into Kanab Canyon a half mile or so. The

creek was no more than a clear, bubbling brook. Yet it is a major tributary, with its source in Utah more than a hundred miles to the north, and over the eons it has carved a sensational winding gorge which at its lower end is a Grand Canyon in miniature. Miniature is perhaps the wrong word, for it is just as deep as the big river's: its wrinkled pink inner walls towered nearly 1,500 feet above my head. But it was far narrower. Barely two hundred feet separated the base of the opposite walls at the point which I reached, and I knew that farther up the canyon narrowed in places to forty feet.

I sat down on a rock by the edge of the creek, and absorbed the splendor and serenity of this lost canyon. Two hundred yards downstream Kanab Creek turned to the left, and there the cliffs were bathed in sun. The shaded waters of the creek reflected the bright colors of the rocks, and a snowy egret stalked through the shimmering reflections. Presently the big bird took flight, its long neck and legs outstretched, and as it banked into the sunlight it was a sudden dazzling flash of white. From up the gorge tumbled the song of a canyon wren— that haunting, disembodied song which to me had become the voice of the canyons, just as the coyote's howl was the voice of the desert. It seemed to say, "Follow me, follow me," and I was sorely tempted to do so. I was almost willing to eschew the balance of the river trip in order to explore fully this glorious Kanab Canyon, where every bend teases you into wanting to discover what further beauty lies around it. And I promised myself that before long I would return, with a pack on my back and time on my hands.

I would return, that is, unless the engineers of the City of Los Angeles and of the Bureau of Reclamation got there first. For if they had their way Kanab Canyon would be vandalized.

The Kanab Creek Diversion Project, or Kanab Tunnel Plan, as it is variously called, was described by the Bureau in its voluminous 1946 report on the economic development resources of the Colorado River, and has since been vigorously championed by some kilowatt-hungry individuals in Los Angeles. The report points out that the Colorado River drops approximately 1,260 feet in the 150 miles between Glen Canyon Dam site in the upper basin and the estimated normal water surface of the proposed Bridge Canyon Reservoir. And it suggests that "to develop fully the power possibilities of the Colorado River and yet avoid the construction of dams or other works in the Grand Canyon National Park, Colorado River waters not needed to maintain a steady stream for scenic purposes in the park could be diverted

ANSEL ADAMS: View northeast from near Yaki Point

Never static, never still, inconstant as the passing moment and yet endurable as time itself, it is the one great drama of evolutionary change perpetually recapitulated. Yet the canyon refutes even this geological reality. In its depths whole mountains contract and expand with the changing shadows.

FRANK WATERS

through a tunnel 44.8 miles long to a power plant near the mouth of Kanab Creek. With an installed capacity of 1,250,000 kilowatts this Kanab Creek power plant operating under an average head of about 1,100 feet could produce 6.5 billion kilowatt-hours of firm energy annually."

A dam 470 feet high would be built in Kanab Creek, impounding a reservoir of 65,000 acre feet of water. An underground powerhouse 90 feet wide, 105 feet high, and 880 feet long would be installed near the mouth of Kanab Creek, and access roads would be built to the dam and the powerhouse. All these features of the plan—as well as the dumping of excavated materials—would be immediately adjacent to the present minimal Grand Canyon National Park, which is across the river from the mouth of Kanab Creek, but would be within the critical area of what could be a comprehensive park.

The tunnel would pass through Grand Canyon National Park for about five miles in the vicinity of Tapeats Creek, and an adit would emerge at Tapeats Creek for the dumping of tunnel spoil. The excavated material removed from this adit and from the aqueduct through the adit would amount to 2.5 million cubic yards, and would be released near the adit entrance in Grand Canyon National Park. An access road would be required within the Park to reach this adit, and construction facilities, necessarily located within the Park, would be required at the adit for cement and aggregate handling and storage, a concrete mixing plant, and buildings to house maintenance shops and offices.

Every one of these features would be in direct violation of the 1916 National Parks Act, which requires that the scenery and other natural and historic objects within the parks be preserved unimpaired for the enjoyment of future generations. The wilderness atmosphere of the Park would be irreparably impaired at great distances from the encroachments themselves. But most serious of all would be the effect of the plan on the river in the Park. The tunnel would divert 91 per cent of the flow of the river, leaving a puny stream of 1,000 cubic feet per second to follow the river channel through the Park. This would be analogous to logging 91 per cent of Sequoia National Park, and leaving a "representative" 9 per cent to placate those who cared.

In a brief filed with the Federal Power Commission on April 9, 1962, the National Parks Association stated: "The diversion of 91 per cent of the flow of the Colorado River would be disastrous to the purpose of Grand Canyon National Park and Monument. The number of people who have descended the Bright Angel Trail from the south rim, or have gone down from Kaibab Plateau on the north rim to the river, and have seen its tremendous sweep and power, must now, as a matter of history, be indeed considerable. Countless Americans have been deeply impressed by the sight of this powerful river in Grand Canyon National Park. As a result, they are better able to comprehend the immense length of time required to carve out the great canyon through the deep rocks, and, in addition, to better understand the vast geological time involved in the deposition of the rocks themselves. These are matters of great spiritual value to the human race in understanding its relationship to the cosmos. To reduce the Colorado River through the Grand Canyon Park to 'a mere trickle,' as proposed in the Kanab Tunnel Plan, would be a defilement; only such minds as are confined in their perspective to the material exploitation of the continent at all costs, as against cultural values, could countenance such a proposal."

Unfortunately, it appears that such minds dominate the Bureau of Reclamation. In May 1949, supporting the firm opposition of the National Park Service to the Kanab diversion project, Assistant Secretary of the Interior William E. Warne directed the Bureau of Reclamation to halt all investigation of the plan. The Bureau overtly complied—so far as is known it has carried out no field investigation of the potential diversion since 1949. But it is only biding its time, as was made clear in 1957. With the concurrence of the Forest Service, the National Park Service had formulated plans to add to the Grand Canyon National Park 42,265 acres on the north side of Grand Canyon between Grand Canyon National Monument and Tapeats Creek, including several miles of Kanab Creek Canyon. On January 17, 1957, Senator Barry Goldwater of Arizona introduced legislation in Congress which would have revised the National Park's boundaries to include this area as well as two smaller ones on the south rim. However, the Bureau of Reclamation objected, stating that "further consideration [of the Marble Gorge-Kanab Creek Project] should not be effectively foreclosed by including the site of the power plant within the boundaries of a National Park." The Bureau, which ranks with the Army Corps of Engineers as a prime mover and executor of pork-barrel projects, generally has the ear of Congress, and the Goldwater bill got nowhere. Los Angeles is still pushing for the Kanab Creek diversion project; the threatened area is still outside the Park; and we may still see the day when the only reminder of the river whose power cut the Grand Canyon will be an anemic trickle.

. . . The scenery of the amphitheaters far surpasses in grandeur and nobility anything else of the kind in any other region, but it is mere by-play in
comparison with the panorama displayed in the heart of the canyon. The
supreme views are to be obtained at the extremities of the long promontories,
which jut out between these recesses far into the gulf . . .

CLARENCE E. DUTTON

CLYDE THOMAS: Beach at Spring Canyon, Mile 204.4

10. Whitmore Wash

THE WEATHER grew steadily warmer during the day as we proceeded downriver from Kanab Creek. The cloudless sky was a deep, postcard blue, and the red limestone walls on either side of us soared toward it in an alternation of cliffs and talus slopes. The latter were a smoky green with sparse desert vegetation: barrel cacti, agave, yuccas, nolinas or Indian soapweed with tall creamy plumes. For the first time we saw some ocotillo, coachwhips with flamelike cones of flowers at their tips. Much of the time the cliffs plunged straight to the river, as they had in parts of Marble Gorge, and as we drifted by we admired the texture of the river-sculptured rock.

The left shore was still in the National Park. From a mile below Kanab Creek the right shore formed the south boundary of the Grand Canyon National Monument. But there was another aspect of the local geography of which I was well aware. Just below Kanab Creek we had passed the point where the river's elevation was 1,866 feet above sea level. And that was to be the normal water level of the reservoir impounded by the proposed Bridge Canyon Dam. If the dam were built, the flowing river, however vestigial the Bureau left it, would end at Kanab Creek; the next ninety-three miles of its course through the Grand Canyon would be another man-made lake. Every mile we now traveled would be deeper under water; with every mile, more of the canyon walls would be submerged; with every mile, more of the side canyons would be drowned. This knowledge, insistent as a tocsin, colored my feelings as it had in Marble Gorge.

We were rowing close to the left-hand wall about four in the afternoon when the *Susie Too* ahead of us turned suddenly to port, headed straight for the wall—and disappeared. We followed down to the point at which it had veered, and came to what for me was the biggest surprise of the Canyon. A narrow cleft slit the cliff from top to bottom, and out of it flowed Havasu Creek. One second we were rowing on the coffee-brown Colorado, the next we were floating on water which was a swimming-pool blue. The passage was just wide enough in spots for the boats to get through, and the walls were even closer together above us, frequently overhanging the creek. The water was clear as a Caribbean lagoon, and big carp loafed along the white limey bottom. A wind-ing series of tubs or basins led us, after fifty yards or so, to a wider pool at the back of which a low cataract foamed. We could see a short way up Havasu Canyon, boxed in by towering yellow and red cliffs. There was something quite unreal about the entrance of Havasu Creek. It reminded me of nothing I had ever seen, except vaguely, perhaps, photographs of the Blue Grotto at Capri.

This was one of the smaller but brighter gems of the Grand Canyon National Park, and yet, if the dam were built, the mouth of Havasu Creek would be under eighty-five feet of water. How was this desecration compatible with the national policy, backed by law, to preserve "unimpaired" the scenery of the National Parks and Monuments?

It was not, and the proponents of Bridge Canyon Dam have admitted as much. In forwarding to Secretary Udall the Bureau of Reclamation's Pacific Southwest Water Plan, which calls for erection of Bridge and Marble dams, Assistant Secretary of the Interior for Water and Power Development Kenneth Holum wrote: "During development of the Initial Plan, I have not been unmindful of your concern regarding impact of any proposed developments upon Grand Canyon National Park and Grand Canyon National Monument. The high dam at Bridge Canyon would back water some 93 miles; first, 53 miles within Lake Mead National Recreation Area; then 27 miles where the Monument includes or borders the river; and, finally, the last 13 miles of the reservoir would abut the Park along the Colorado River and extend a distance of less than one mile into the Park at Havasu Creek." And Udall, testifying before the Senate Subcommittee on Irrigation and Reclamation, declared that "It is a well-established policy of the Federal Government to preserve as nearly as possible the natural conditions within national parks and monuments. . . . In terms of [these] principles, the creation of a man-made lake on a 13-mile stretch in the National Park would 'impair the scenic beauty' of the Grand Canyon National Park.

"However," Udall continued, "it should be noted that such a reservoir invasion would be a peripheral one which would occur in the most remote and inaccessible area of the park. It should be further noted that 98 per cent of the land area in the park would remain in its natural condition." This argument is a most insidious one. There is probably not a single National Park in the country where economic justification could not be found for a "peripheral invasion" of one kind or another. Allow such an infringement in one park, for instance Grand Canyon National Park, and it would become increasingly difficult to prevent others elsewhere. The precedent would have been set. A process of erosion would set in, and the addition of new parks to the National Park System—perhaps a Redwoods National Park, or a Canyonlands or a Northern Cascades National Park—would in no way compensate for the invasion of the older units. For the new parks would be subject to the same attrition if it were once allowed to attack Grand Canyon National Park. A further argument of Udall's in support of Bridge Canyon Dam points this up: "It must also be recognized," he told the Senate subcommittee, "that the pristine natural condition of the river has already been permanently altered by the construction of upstream dams which regulate the flow of the river and control its spring floods. These are the river forces which, over the eons of time, have carved out the majestic chasm that is now the Grand Canyon." In other words, the building of Glen Canyon Dam already constituted an infringement of Grand Canyon National Park, and since it was allowed it justified further infringement by the Bridge Canyon reservoir which would merely compound the harm. The Secretary could not have given a clearer demonstration of the way any violation of the integrity of a National Park can establish the precedent for later violations. In view of this, could anyone still argue that those who would preserve our National Park System can afford to compromise and to be what some developers call reasonable?

But the principal argument adduced by the Secretary and the reclamationists in defense of Bridge Canyon Dam is that the act establishing the Park specifically authorized such a project, and that, to quote Mr. Udall, "such a development was foreseen and acquiesced in by those who prepared the proclamation" of the National Monument. The pertinent section of the Grand Canyon National Park Organic Act of February 26, 1919, provides that "Whenever consistent with the primary purposes of said park, the Secretary of the Interior is authorized to permit the utilization of areas therein which may be necessary for the development and maintenance of government reclamation projects."

The phrasing of this section is of the greatest significance. On May 16, 1918, Senate Bill 390, from which the Grand Canyon Act was derived, was considered on the floor of the Senate. The Bill was reported from the Committee on Public Lands with the bare provision that the Reclamation Service might utilize areas within the Park where necessary for a reclamation project. The Bill was then amended by the insertion of the phrase "whenever consistent with the primary purposes of the said park." This amendment, in effect, nullified the reclamation provision. For no reclamation project could be developed which would be "consistent with the primary purposes of said park"—the primary purposes being, as defined by the National Parks Act of 1916, "to conserve the scenery and the natural and historic objects and the wildlife therein, and to provide for the enjoyment of the same in such manner and by such means as will leave them unimpaired for the enjoyment of future generations." The insistence upon the language came from an earlier Secretary of the Interior.*

Bridge Canyon reservoir would destroy some of the finest scenery in the Park and Monument, would destroy the natural objects therein, would destroy or displace the wildlife, and would leave the area permanently impaired for future generations.

But surely, some overweening national interest must dictate the building of the dam even at the price of endangering the whole National Park and Monument System. Surely this must be a case where no alternatives exist. Surely, at the very least, Bridge Canyon dam is "necessary for the development and maintenance of government reclamation projects." No. Only by an exercise in semantics could the Pacific Southwest Water Plan be termed a reclamation project. And only by ignoring readily available alternatives could Bridge Canyon and Marble Gorge dams be considered necessary for the development of the Water Plan. We would be reminded of this shortly.

The sun had disappeared over the rim by the time we emerged from Havasu Canyon, and we rowed only another mile or two downriver before landing on the right bank for the night. The air was still and balmy, and after supper I lay on top of my sleeping bag, watching the swarms of bats flitter overhead. The stars blinked on one by one in the narrow ribbon of sky contained between the Canyon walls, and I plotted their westward progress using for reference points the "stone babies" on

---

* *The reader who wishes to delve deeper into the legal, technical, economic and political aspects of the Bridge Canyon and Marble Gorge dam proposals is referred to the expert analyses in the Appendices to this book.*

CLYDE CHILDRESS: *Shore by Hermit Rapid, Mile 94.9*

I suppose that nothing living had moved among those great stones for centuries. They lay toppled against each other like fallen dolmens. The huge stones were beasts, I used to think, of a kind man ordinarily lived too fast to understand. They seemed inanimate because the tempo of the life in them was slow. They lived ages in one place and moved only when man was not looking. Sometimes at night I would hear a low rumble as one drew itself into a new position and subsided again. Sometimes I found their tracks ground deeply into the hillsides.   LOREN EISELEY the rim—the erect monoliths which Havasupai mothers warn their children they will be turned into if they are naughty. When it was really night, and I had slipped into my bag with the warm sand for a mattress and my life jacket for a pillow, I noticed one star that seemed to be a rebel. It was moving slowly *up* the Canyon, east northeast, in the opposite direction from the rest. Then it dawned on me that this was no star but a man-made satellite, and I wondered if there were a man aboard it— perhaps one of my recent companions on the hike down the Kaibab Trail. If so I wished him luck—he was far more isolated than we were, and dependent for his survival on the flawless functioning of his machine. In this respect the spaceman seemed to me to be a symbol of our age—the age of the machine, the age in which the machine had ceased to be our servant and became increasingly our master. I thought of the tyranny of the automobile. Machines in automated plants displacing the skilled worker. Electronic computers shaping political decisions, if Eugene Burdick was to be believed. And as we grew ever more dependent on the machine, a Frankenstein's monster with microcircuits for brains, we were increasingly estranged from the natural world which had spawned us. Paul B. Sears had warned, "As we lengthen and elaborate the chain of technology that intervenes between us and the natural world, we . . . become steadily more vulnerable to even the slightest failure in that chain." It was easy to forget this, insulated as most of us were in our urban cocoons. But a week or two in the wilderness usually sufficed to restore a man's sense of proportion, to remind him that he was no demigod but a warmblooded mammal dependent, like the rest, on the products of photosynthesis and the march of the seasons, that the tides ebbed and flowed independent of his will and that the weather, thank God, was still beyond his control. We needed every vestige of our primeval wilderness, we needed our parks not merely for recreation but as an antidote to megalomania. I was as fascinated as the next fellow by the exploration of space. But I would not exchange one acre of national park for any number of airless moonports.

We were up and about the next morning before the sun hit the top of the downstream cliff. It was another cloudless day, with a breeze gently ruffling the tamarisks, and we were on the river by eight; a few minutes later a white egret, motionless on a beach, watched us drift by. A little farther down we flushed some blue-winged teal, and they sped downriver ahead of us, their wingtips barely missing the water, almost riding on the echoes of their downstrokes. We came to a long stretch in which

the base of the left wall had been carved into a frieze of Mayan profiles, Palenque or Chichén Itzá on a heroic scale. These effects of the flowing river on the streamside rocks were endlessly varied and endlessly fascinating— but doomed, of course, should there ever be a Bridge Canyon dam.

Between Kanab Creek and Parashont Wash, fifty-five river miles, the Colorado headed generally west southwest, but with innumerable twists and turns. This was not the typical course of a fast-running stream which still had nearly two thousand feet to drop before it reached the sea. It was more like the course of a lazy, spent river nearing its encounter with the ocean. But that is exactly what the Colorado had been before the land rose beneath it. Had the land lifted faster than it did, the river would have been dumped from its bed and would have sought a straighter, faster channel. But this had not happened, and the river still flowed in its ancient channel, which now ran thousands of feet below the general level of the land, a classic example of an entrenched meander.

In the curve of one of the meanders we ran a small rapid and landed on the right shore. From a wide sandy beach crossed by a bobcat's tracks I walked back into Fern Glen, a miniature Eden perhaps two hundred yards long cradled between vertical red cliffs. House finches were chirruping in the catclaws, abloom with yellow catkins, that bordered the dry streambed. But the stream was only dry at its lower end. I turned a corner, and at the foot of an immense boulder that blocked the passage found a small pool of clear water. More water was seeping from the walls of the canyon, and they were tapestried with ferns through which peeped the startling scarlet flowers of mimulus. A stairstep ledge allowed me to climb to the next level of the little canyon. Here a thin thread of running water connected a series of tiny pools on the gravelly floor, and at the back of the chamber a trickle ran down a twenty foot high travertine tongue built out from the lip of the water notch in the Muav ledge. The travertine was in fact a petrified waterfall: each drop of water that evaporated against it added its tiny load of lime to the tongue. I could not climb this ledge, but I could tell there was a still higher pool by the reflections playing against the sides of its rock bowl. The left wall of Fern Glen was thickly hung with maidenhair and, as I noticed when I looked more closely, with stream-orchids, their petals a pale yellow delicately veined with brown and green. I stood in the quiet of this delightful spot, sheltered from the din of the river by Fern Glen's winding walls,

Around on the rocks in the cavelike chamber are set beautiful ferns, with delicate fronds and enameled stalks. The frondlets have their points turned down to form spore cases. It has very much the appearance of the maidenhair fern, but is much larger. This delicate foliage covers the rocks all about the fountain, and gives the chamber great beauty. . . .

JOHN WESLEY POWELL

CLYDE CHILDRESS: Fern Glen, Mile 168.0

and had I stayed there long enough could easily have forgotten that I was in the Grand Canyon. I thought back to Vasey's Paradise, Elves' Chasm, Deer Creek—the immensity of the Canyon setting imparted pathos to the delicate beauty of such places, and they, in turn, sharpened one's awareness of the Canyon's majesty. Such contrasts gave added richness and meaning to the Grand Canyon experience, but they would be harder to come by if the dams were built. Fern Glen, like Vasey's, would be drowned.

After lunching on the beach, we took to the boats. We now were enjoying typical Southwest desert weather. The sun burned fiercely in a cobalt sky, and by two in the afternoon the thermometer in the *Susie Too* registered 96° in the shade. The heat was pleasantly stupefying; the boatmen rowed no more than they had to, and the rest of us just basked sleepily in the sun. We made camp early, landing in a cove on the right bank just upstream from Toroweap overlook. I did as desert animals do on a hot afternoon—I holed up in the shade of a tamarisk and drowsed, not really asleep but my mind blanked out, and only my senses alive to the feel of sand and of heat and the gurgling of the river at my feet. The Canyon wall across the river, vaulting skyward in a series of gigantic leaps, was as stupendous as ever, but I was not looking at it with the eyes of a human, gauging and measuring and associating and admiring. I was seeing with the eyes of an animal, half-closed, registering only the texture of sunlit rock and the flutter of a mourning dove from one mesquite to another. I ceased for a while to be an outsider; my internal rhythm slowed to that of my surroundings; I was in tune with the Canyon, as much a part of it as the tamarisk under which I lay. Such moments are precious, and their after-image lingers on even after one's brain has switched back to its normal wave length.

Later, when we were having supper, a foreign sound intruded suddenly on the peace of the Canyon. It grew louder quickly, and soon we saw, heading towards us from downriver and flying at about the level of the rim, a yellow Piper Cub. As it passed three thousand feet overhead, looking at that distance like a bright little insect, the pilot dropped a shiny object out the window, which landed high on the unscalable Canyon wall across the river. Pat Reilly recognized the plane as that of John Riffey, Custodian of Grand Canyon National Monument, and Riffey apparently had tried to drop us a message. We thought perhaps he would make another run by but he did not—presumably the Canyon updrafts were too rough to allow the little plane to make a lower and more accurate pass. But after dark we spotted a light blinking at us from Toroweap. We surmised this was Riffey again (we later found out it was), and wondered if he was merely being sociable or was trying to warn us of something. I had a premonition of trouble ahead, but in the calm of this velvet evening I found it impossible to worry. This was a fine camp, with clean level sand on which to lie and nothing left to do but to gaze at the stars. Something, perhaps a Canyon toad, went "cheep, cheep, cheep" near my head, a sweet, rather questioning little voice.

There would be no more campsites like this if the dam were built; no graceful sandy beaches, no shade of tamarisk or willow or mesquite in which to seek shelter from the burning sun. "A fresh water lake could provide boat-type access to a region of park that would otherwise be available for only the most limited use," Secretary Udall had told the Senate. But aside from the fact that motorboats are as inadmissible in National Parks as trail scooters, boating on the Marble Gorge and Bridge Canyon reservoirs would be like boating in giant bathtubs. Along most of their shorelines vertical walls would offer no landings; at best would-be campers would find uncomfortable ledges on steep talus slopes and these, if one can make predictions from recent experience in Glen Canyon, would soon be a mess of cans, papers, plastic containers and uncovered toilet areas. Sailing would be hazardous if not impossible; waterskiers would have but two directions in which to go—upstream or downstream; the tall cliffs would echo and magnify the noise of the motorboats. For boating enthusiasts, of which I am one, the reservoir would be far inferior to Lake Mead just downstream. For those who knew Marble Gorge and the lower Grand Canyon when they were still wilderness, the reservoirs would be a desecration. Even from the point of view of recreationists, Roosevelt's plea for the Canyon rang true: "Leave it as it is. You cannot improve on it. The ages have been at work on it, and man can only mar it."

Dawn broke warm and clear, and an early alpenglow lit Toroweap overlook, fading slowly as the day grew lighter. Before we pushed off, we again noticed a light flashing at us from the point. It was Riffey again (as we confirmed later), signaling to us, this time with a mirror. Our suspicions rearoused, we nevertheless took to the boats, and within minutes came to an enormous boulder that towered at least fifty feet high in midstream, a compact mass of black basalt crystals. It would be hard to imagine an environment less hospitable to life than this isolated rock, yet its top was capped with prickly pear and barrel cacti. This was Vulcan's Forge, the first evidence to meet our eyes of the extraordinary vulcanism in the next section of the Canyon.

About a mile below Vulcan's Forge we began to hear the thunder of a major rapid, which grew louder as we approached. Then we saw, perched on the very brink of the north rim, the cinder cone of Vulcan's Throne. From this volcano and other sources a great stream of molten lava had poured down into the river, congealing against the canyon wall. "What a conflict of water and fire there must have been here!" Powell had written. "Just imagine a river of molten rock, running down into a river of melted snow. What a seething and boiling of the waters; what clouds of steam rolled into the heavens!" The lava, in cooling, had formed a gigantic dam, perhaps as much as fifteen hundred feet high—which would have backed up the Colorado's waters all the way to the site of modern-day Lee's Ferry, 180 miles upstream.

Over the broken basaltic rocks which were all that now remained of the dam the river poured in a furious rapid—the formidable Lava Falls. We landed just above it on the left bank, flushing two great blue herons in the process, and walked down the wide gravel fan at the mouth of Prospect Canyon to look over the rapid. Immediately below the initial drop a great wave, like a surf breaker, stretched across the whole river. Behind it a deep trough, and another huge, curling comber. Then a mad confusion of holes and explosion waves and jagged protruding rocks. There was no practicable channel through this turmoil, and although Lava Falls has been successfully run at certain stages of water it was obvious that we could not run it this day. We had to portage, which took us until noon, then had lunch in a grove of tamarisks near a travertine spring. We reloaded the boats and pushed off about one o'clock, immediately running lower Lava Falls and taking on some water in the process. But the sun was sizzling and getting wet a pleasure.

We drifted on down past mile after mile of lava which coated sometimes the north wall of the Canyon, sometimes the south, sometimes both. The basalt frequently had a fine columnar structure. In places the columns were vertical, in others they were slanting or curved. Sometimes they formed a rosette radiating from a central point, and one formation took the shape of a gigantic, perfectly shaped seashell. Devil's Postpile National Monument had been established near Yosemite National Park to preserve a similar basaltic cliff, sixty feet high and three hundred yards long. Here in the Grand Canyon these formations stretched for miles—and yet the dam builders were quite prepared to submerge them.

We passed Whitmore Wash on the right, where a trail zigzags up the lava to the rim, at three in the afternoon and stopped to camp on the right shore a half mile below it. We were tired from the portage at Lava Falls and the heat of the afternoon and glad to call it a day. An hour later we heard the drone of a plane approaching from downstream. It came into view around a bend, flying low, a small white National Park Service plane. As it passed overhead the pilot dropped what appeared to be a message in a plastic bag. The object fell in the river and was lost. The plane came by a second time, dropping yet another bag. This one I fished out of the water, and in it found a typewritten page, which read:

Lake Mead National Recreational Area
Boulder City, Nevada, May 12, 1964

P. T. Reilly River Party:

The gates of Glen Canyon Dam were closed yesterday morning (May 11). The river flow has been cut to 1,000 cfs. It is important that you leave the river by Whitmore Canyon. If you agree three of you wave something white the next time we pass. Others remain away from the three and remain quiet. If you concur by waving we will notify persons on your permit to meet you at the end of the Whitmore Canyon road.

(signed) James W. Packard
Chief Park Ranger

If you receive this note and do not wish to leave the river, one person stand alone and wave something white.   J. W. P.

And handwritten: "Lee's Ferry run off this morning 1,000 cfs. Grand Canyon run off this AM 9,000 cfs."

This, then, was what Riffey had been trying to warn us about. We held a brief council of war on the beach. Leaving by Whitmore Wash, which we had already passed, would mean abandoning the boats where they were, along with most of our gear and supplies, and hiking back along the river to the foot of the Whitmore Wash trail, which we were not certain it was possible to do. On the other hand, if we continued downstream and the river dropped beneath us to 1,000 cubic feet per second we were likely to be stranded. We would encounter places too shallow for the boats to float across, and every rapid and riffle would be an impossible boulder field which we would have to line or portage. What tipped the scales was the information that the flow at Bright Angel that morning was still 9,000 cfs. This meant that we would probably have runnable water for another twenty-four hours. If in that time we could reach Separation Canyon, fifty-one miles away, we would be in the clear—from there on all the rapids had been silted over when the level of Lake Mead was high. The Grand

CLYDE THOMAS: Mouth of Whitmore Wash, Mile 188.0

Canyon extends for another forty miles to Grapevine Wash, near Pierce Ferry, but from Separation Canyon on we would be essentially on Lake Mead. Our decision was unanimous. "Let's flush on down," somebody said, and this became our war cry for the rest of the trip, our cry in defiance of the dam builders, of the Bureau of Reclamation, of the whole Philistine cabal of Grand Canyon spoilers. When the Park Service plane flew over again to learn our decision, Martin Litton literally tore his white shirt off his back and, standing well away from the rest of us, waved it triumphantly over his head. The plane rocked in acknowledgment and disappeared.

Within minutes we had broken camp, reloaded the boats and pushed off. And there was no dawdling on the river now, no drifting with the current, no photography stops. Our one thought was to put as many miles behind us as possible before daylight failed us. For more than two hours the boatmen rowed without letup, and when we put into shore below Parashont Wash we had added a dozen miles to our day's run.

Our conversation at dinner, naturally enough, revolved around the closing of the gates at Glen Canyon Dam. We did not envy Secretary Udall his job.

Early in 1963, the Secretary had ordered the closing of the gates at Glen Canyon Dam so that the filling of Lake Powell could begin. At the time, he had been quite properly attacked by conservationists for beginning the filling without having taken "adequate protective measures to preclude impairment of Rainbow Bridge National Monument," as he was required to do by the Act authorizing the Colorado River Storage Project.

By March, 1964, Lake Powell had impounded only half of the 6.1 million acre feet necessary to begin the generation of power at the dam. (An acre foot is a volume sufficient to cover one acre with one foot of water.) At the same time, Lake Mead had dropped to 1,123 feet elevation, below which power output at Hoover Dam would be cut. And the forecast was for a low spring runoff in the Colorado River Basin. Weighing all these factors, Mr. Udall ordered the opening of the gates at Glen Canyon Dam in order to maintain elevation 1,123 at Lake Mead. This decision set off an immediate uproar in the Upper Basin States of Wyoming, Colorado, Utah, and New Mexico. Senator Wallace F. Bennett (Rep.-Utah) demanded that Mr. Udall "stop the Interior Department's water pirating policy." Former Colorado Governor and U.S. Senator Ed C. Johnson described the decision to lower Lake Powell as "arbitrary, dictatorial, positively unnecessary and perfectly stupid." Felix Sparks, director of the Colorado Water

Conservation Board, threatened that "it may be necessary for Upper Basin states to determine once and for all through the courts whether they must remain forever in bondage to power contractors at Hoover Dam." The governors of all four states signed a letter of protest to Mr. Udall, and Governor John A. Love of Colorado threatened court action, charging that the Secretary "is completely disregarding the provisions of the Colorado River Compact and the law of the river is being junked."

What additional pressures Secretary Udall may have been subjected to from within his own department, i.e., from the Bureau of Reclamation, can only be surmised. But obviously Lake Powell must be filled at almost all costs and Glen Canyon Dam must begin to generate electricity, or the American taxpayer might want to examine more closely the Bureau's grandiose plans for maximum development of the Colorado River. And such scrutiny might prove fatal to the Bureau's empire-building dreams. We had been assured in advance that although the Secretary would announce on May 11 the intent to close the gates, the actual closing would be delayed until May 15, allowing us time to finish our schedule as planned. At any rate, on May 11, the Glen Canyon Dam gates were closed, allowing only 1,000 cubic feet per second to run down to Lake Mead. And this was the order which had put us on the spot.

Our predicament, of course, was of little consequence. But the order was a blow to a good many interests in the Lower Basin (California, Arizona and Nevada) and Mexico, and was aggravated by a further order that Lower Basin users of Colorado River water cut their diversions by ten per cent. Once again the Secretary was deluged with complaints. "The Udall order of a 10 per cent cut in water uses in the Lower Basin does not reflect an actual drought situation," said M. J. Dowd, Colorado River Commissioner of California. "The order reflects an artificial crisis, a Udall illusion intended to gratify interests related only to power generation, Upper Basin interests which are careless of urban and irrigation needs of people living in the Lower Basin of the river. . . . The Udall order . . . comes without warning to irrigators and ignores crop patterns now in progress as a result of careful planning by growers who relied upon contractual promises and who cannot shift operations impulsively." Robert A. Skinner, general manager and chief engineer of the Metropolitan Water District of Los Angeles, charged that "the Secretary has ignored the clear principle that the impounding of water for the generation of power must remain subservient to the use of such water for domestic and agricultural purposes."

Secretary Udall had sought to allay Lower Basin interests' fears by specifying that under no circumstances would Lake Mead be dropped below 1,083 feet elevation (the minimum elevation for power generation at Hoover Dam), and guaranteeing that the Bureau of Reclamation would purchase power on the open market and thereby furnish "replacement capacity and energy to the Hoover power allottees in the same quantities and having the same characteristics they would have obtained from Lake Mead operating at elevation 1,123." But this looked like dubious economics. Said Samuel B. Nelson, general manager and chief engineer of the Los Angeles City Department of Water and Power, the agency with which the Bureau contracts to operate the public power generators at Hoover Dam: "The Udall order to sequester so much water back of Glen Canyon Dam, out of which this water will come hard if a real drought develops, has by no means proven to be the most profitable way to manage power production on the river. To reduce production of 18 electrical generators at Hoover Dam in order to start one at Glen Canyon, and months later another there, and months later a third—maybe—is supposed to be supported by Federal figures which are yet to be given for checking by engineers who advise other interested public agencies. When we receive these data as now promised, and analyze them, more detailed comment may be made on this financial aspect of the power situation. As of now, we are skeptical."

In essence, Mr. Udall had gambled that Lake Powell could be filled to 6.1 million acre feet before Lake Mead dropped below its minimum power-generating capacity of 10.7 million acre feet (its capacity at 1,083 feet elevation.) But even if the gamble were to pay off in 1964, there was no assurance that the gain would be permanent. "Another hazard involved here," Mr. Udall had admitted, "is that, even though Lake Powell may go into operation at its minimum level, the runoff next spring could be so low as again to require the lowering of Lake Powell beyond the minimum operating head in order to keep Lake Mead at even a minimum level. In this event, the Government may well be obligated to buy power at the expense of the Upper Basin fund to supply its Upper Basin power sales contracts as well as the Hoover power allottees." In studies which had led to the formulation of the criteria for the filling of Lake Powell, it had been recognized that a succession of dry years might mean that it would take up to *twenty years* to fill Lake Powell. Twenty years during which Glen Canyon Dam would produce less than the planned power. Twenty years during which this supposedly self-liquidating venture would produce inadequate revenues to pay for itself or for the "participating projects"—projects to provide water for irrigation and for municipal and industrial uses. Twenty years during which the financing of the participating projects could have been assured if reliance had been placed on revenue not from hydropower but from thermal power, production of which would not have depended on the vagaries of the weather, and would not have required the permanent defacement of Glen Canyon's beauty or the flagrant breach by The Bureau of its promise to protect Rainbow Bridge National Monument and of the law requiring protection.

And now, despite the lesson being learned at Lake Powell, the Bureau of Reclamation proposed to build two more huge dams on the Colorado within the Grand Canyon, at Marble Gorge and Bridge Canyon. How would the Bureau obtain the water to fill these reservoirs? By again dumping Lake Powell?

The basic problem, of course, was that the states of the Colorado River Basin were trying to develop and divide more water than was available. The Colorado River Compact of 1922 had apportioned to each of the upper and lower basins in perpetuity a total of 7,500,000 acre feet a year for beneficial consumptive use, and had stipulated that the states of the Upper Division could not cause the flow of the Colorado River at Lee's Ferry to be depleted below an aggregate of 75,000,000 acre feet for any period of ten consecutive years. Based on the average river flow for the previous 25 years, this was a reasonable agreement. However, tree-ring studies have since shown that precipitation during those 25 years was abnormally high—in fact it may have been the wettest 25-year cycle in one thousand years.

This was the hydrologically not-so-mighty Colorado. This was the river which was scheduled to provide 7,500,000 acre feet a year to the Upper Basin, 7,500,000 acre feet a year to the Lower Basin, 1,500,000 acre feet a year to Mexico (under the Treaty of 1944), and to fill the reservoirs behind Glen Canyon, Marble Gorge and Bridge Canyon dams, and Lake Mead, Lake Mojave, Lake Havasu,—and was also to seep in part into the dark lakes leading no one knew where, and to vanish into the invisible lake of the atmosphere through evaporation enough, in the aggregate Bureau plan for this arid land, to supply water for ten Denvers and ten Phoenixes. This was engineering unmitigated, coupled with the destruction of examples of earth sculpture as magnificent as man has known; no engineering could replace them.

DAVID R. BROWER: Lake Mead at Hoover Dam

PHILIP HYDE: Silt near Grand Wash Cliffs, ca. Mile 281

The sedge is wither'd from the lake,
  And no birds sing.

KEATS

The time has come in America for a fresh appraisal of the function of the engineer in our society. This man who is the designer and builder of our habitat —this man who above all others sets the stage for our daily lives—should anticipate the impact of each project he plans upon the total evolution of America. Without such awareness the disorderly pattern of the present man-made environment will be compounded as the pressures of population density increase.

EDWARD HIGBEE

CLYDE THOMAS: Spencer Canyon silt, Lake Mead, Mile 246

DAVID R. BROWER: Picnic area at Pierce Ferry, Mile 274.9

11. Separation Canyon

WE AROSE in the morning at first light, and noticed at once that the river had dropped eighteen inches overnight. We took this as a warning and by six o'clock we were afloat. Before an hour was out we landed on the left shore above Two Hundred and Five Mile Rapid. Two white egrets took off as we approached, and we noted fresh beaver tracks leading from the river to a ledge fifteen feet away. Four pencil-sized willow stumps were additional evidence of the beavers' presence. And fresh raccoon tracks ran along the water's edge.

The rapid was rough but all three boats ran it without trouble. A few minutes later I took the oars of the *Lucky Pierre*, and I was still rowing when we piled into Granite Park Rapid, a long splashy affair. To my great satisfaction—and that of my passengers—I got through it without shipping water. A few miles farther down I took the oars again, this time through Two Hundred and Seventeen Mile Rapid, and successfully steered the *Lucky Pierre* through some rather rough water. This was a lot better, I decided, than riding through the rapids as a passenger. For one thing I could see where I was going, whereas up to now, owing to the way the boat was loaded, I had been obliged to ride facing upstream, and could only guess at what was coming by the changing expressions on Bill Jones's face.

We spotted more wildlife during the course of the morning than on any other day of the trip. We counted ten wild burros in two different herds, some of them handsomely marked with light gray coats and black vertical shoulder stripes. Five snowy egrets preceded us for a way. A red-tailed hawk soared high along the flank of the Redwall to our right. Two blue-winged teal circled over us and flew away downstream. A pair of antelope ground squirrels scurried with tails high across some boulders on the shore. And Pat Reilly spotted a beaver just as it plunged into the river. What would happen to all these Canyon dwellers, I wondered, if the flowing river were replaced by a man-made lake? The burros would probably adapt, and so of course would the hawk. But what about the water birds? What food could they find in a reservoir's sterile waters? What about the squirrels, and the raccoons, and the beaver? One writer has described a beaver he saw in Glen Canyon, trapped on a rocky shelf by the rising waters of Lake Powell. "Behind him was a sheer wall; in front of him was more water than he knew what to do with—and it was already lapping at his feet. The march of progress does not concern itself with trivia like beavers." The march of progress *does* concern itself, however, with fishhooks and buckshot. The Pacific Southwest Water Plan would "provide necessary facilities for the conservation and development of fish and wildlife, including urgently needed wintering waterfowl habitat in the Pacific Flyway. Public fishing and hunting opportunities will be expanded to meet ever increasing demands." Presumably, once the native wildlife had been drowned or evicted from nearly 150 miles of the inner Grand Canyon, alien fish would be planted—trout and bass which would belong on this part of the Colorado about as much as crocodiles.

By noon we had rowed better than twenty-five miles, and with Separation Canyon only fourteen miles away we began to feel confident. We stopped for lunch at the mouth of Diamond Creek, with the tall pyramidal spire of Diamond Peak looming over us. This would be one place along the shoreline of Bridge Canyon reservoir to which a road could be built and where a boat could be launched.

Our bearing since Parashont Wash had been toward the south, and shortly after our start this morning we had entered the Lower Granite Gorge. At first the schist and granite had been generally low, usually covered by talus slopes thickly grown with barrel cacti, prickly pear, chollas, agave, and ocotillo. In places the ocotillo looked almost as if they had been planted, like trees in an orchard, with ample, even spacing between the plants. Below Diamond Creek the river swung west and then sharply northwest, and we entered a portion of the inner Canyon reminiscent of the Upper Granite Gorge. The somber schist walls grew higher and higher, their steep and jagged profiles reflecting the vertical upwarping of the rock. The low level of the water revealed the full beauty of the streamside fluting; here and there schist boulders protruded above the current, polished and rounded so that they suggested aquatic mammals such as walruses and hippos. Now and then we would note a yellow travertine formation contrasting with the black

Let us go back a moment to the initial problem: the space available in the national parks is not big enough for all who want to use it. But the size of a park is directly related to the manner in which you use it. If you are in a canoe traveling at three miles an hour, the lake on which you are paddling is ten times as long and ten times as broad as it is to the man in a speedboat going thirty. An hour's paddle will take you as far away as an hour in a speedboat—if there are no speedboats. In other words, more people can use the same space with the same results . . . every road that replaces a footpath, every outboard motor that replaces a canoe paddle, shrinks the area of the park.　　PAUL BROOKS schist, and we stopped for a look at Travertine Canyon. An enormous grotto-like chamber had been eroded in the lime deposit by a small clear creek which entered through a skylight at the rear. Below the grotto the creek leapt helter-skelter in a series of cascades bordered with the usual scarlet monkeyflower and with yellow columbine. Of course this, too, was scheduled to be drowned.

We took off again after about an hour, passed Travertine Falls on our left, and noticed four golden eagles soaring high over our heads. Then the river once more commanded our full attention, as we piled into Two Hundred and Thirty-one Mile Rapid, the first of a closely-spaced series of rough stretches of water. In Two Hundred and Thirty-two Mile Rapid, the current in two places drove full force against the rocky projections from the right shore, and the boatmen only avoided them by vigorous rowing in which they could not afford to miss a stroke. Two Hundred and Thirty-four Mile Rapid soon followed, then Bridge Canyon Rapid and Gneiss Canyon Rapid at miles 235 and 235.8. As we bore down on the latter Pat Reilly called out its name as was his habit: "This is Gneiss!" While we were tossing in its waves I wondered what he had meant, as I could see nothing particularly nice about it, and only later, when I saw the name on the map, did I realize my misunderstanding. There was, on second thought, one nice thing about Gneiss: It was the last real rapid on the river. The river level had held up long enough to see us through the rough spots, and now it did not matter if the flow fell to 1,000 cubic feet per second. We might have some difficulty picking out the channel through the silt beds at Pierce Ferry, but we were sure to reach our tow at Lake Mead.

As we continued down, now fully relaxed, I spotted a big male bobcat near the base of the right wall. He worked his way leisurely up the schist from ledge to ledge, stopping now and then to look us over, and after a minute was lost to view. Like the burros and bighorns he had shown no fear: comparatively safe in the Grand Canyon wilderness, these animals may not have known of the destructiveness of man. Certainly the bobcat could not associate the cable stretched across the gorge just downriver from him with any threat to his way of life. And yet that was where exploratory drilling had been carried out during site studies for Bridge Canyon Dam; 673 feet of water would fill the Inner Gorge at the point where we were rowing and the bobcat had been standing. Soon we passed a row of small cabins above the river on the left—the remains of "Bridge City," the Bureau of Reclamation camp used during the 1942 drillings. And

shortly after five o'clock, tired but jubilant at having beaten the drop of the river level, we put in to the right at Separation Canyon—a day's run of thirty-nine miles in eleven hours, fifteen minutes.

Up on the Canyon wall above our camp a bronze plaque had been bolted. It read:

HERE ON AUGUST 28,
1869,
SENECA HOWLAND, O. G. HOWLAND,
AND
WILLIAM H. DUNN
SEPARATED FROM THE ORIGINAL
POWELL PARTY, CLIMBED TO
THE NORTH RIM AND WERE
KILLED BY THE INDIANS.
FOR FURTHER AUTHENTIC
INFORMATION SEE "COLORADO
RIVER CONTROVERSIES"
OBTAINABLE FROM UNIVERSITY
LIBRARIES.
THIS CENOTAPH WAS PLACED
AND DEDICATED IN 1939 BY LATER
COLORADO RIVER VOYAGERS.

Separation Rapid was no longer—it had been silted in because of Lake Mead. But I could imagine the demoralizing effect another Horn or Granite Falls or Hermit or Serpentine would have had on the three ill-fated men, exhausted and half-starved and skeptical by then of Powell's leadership. And Separation Canyon looked inviting enough. At its mouth a lagoon had formed behind a sandbar along the muddy edge of which were fresh coon and coyote tracks. On the border of the lagoon and forming bowers among the sand dunes was a luxuriant growth of tamarisk, and jimson weed was in full bloom with trumpet-shaped flowers six inches in diameter, white suffused with violet. A fault crossed the gorge of the Colorado at this point like the transept of a church, and Separation Canyon ran arrow-straight toward the northeast, where the cliffs of the upper rim shone brilliant in the late afternoon sun. The lure of this escape route from the dark Canyon underworld had been too strong for the Howlands and Dunn; as I walked up Separation Canyon for a short distance after dinner, well fed, just pleasantly tired, and with the challenges of the Colorado River all behind me for this trip, I pictured the three gaunt men slogging ahead of me toward their appointment with an ironic death.

I thought, too, of Major Powell, of his vision for the West, of his sensible, rational suggestions for the settlement of the "lands of the arid region," as he termed them. If Powell had had his way, he would have rewritten the land and water laws of the West, making them conform to the realities of terrain and climate. He would have drawn state lines to reflect the realities of watersheds and river valleys. And he would have prevented

PHILIP HYDE: Separation Canyon, Mile 239.5

settlement of lands where there was not and could not be an adequate water supply.

I wondered what Powell would have thought of the development of the Colorado River in this century, and of the policies and practices of the Bureau of Reclamation which was his brainchild. That he would have approved of Hoover Dam I had no doubts—that one *had* to be built, if only to put an end once and for all to the disastrous floods in the Colorado's lower reaches. But what about Glen Canyon Dam, and the Bureau's insistence on Marble Gorge and Bridge Canyon dams? Stegner, in *Beyond the Hundredth Meridian*, had pondered somewhat the same question: "(Powell) was a democrat to the marrow and he knew enough about Washington to know that federal controls could have their dangers too. He might see, as many conservationists believe they see, a considerable empire-building tendency within the Bureau of Reclamation, an engineer's vision of the West instead of a humanitarian's, a will to build dams without due regard to all the conflicting interests involved. He might fear any bureau that showed less concern with the usefulness of a project than with its effect on the political strength of the bureau. He might join the Sierra Club and other conservation groups in deploring some proposed and 'feasible' dams such as that in Echo Park below the mouth of the Yampa, and he might agree that considerations such as recreation, wildlife protection, preservation for the future of untouched wilderness, might sometimes outweigh possible irrigation and power benefits. He would probably be with those who are already beginning to plead for conservation of reservoir sites themselves, for reservoirs silt up and do not last forever, and men had better look a long way ahead when they begin tampering with natural forces."

What was the rationale behind the Bureau's Marble Gorge and Bridge Canyon projects? Would they, for instance, conserve water?

No.

They would waste water which the region cannot afford to waste. They would waste it in three ways. First, through evaporation. Lake Powell alone, if and when it filled, would evaporate 650,000 acre feet a year, or more than half the additional water which the Pacific Southwest Water Plan was designed to make available to Arizona annually. Marble Gorge and Bridge Canyon reservoirs, together, might evaporate as much as 200,000 acre feet, or twice as much as the Bureau hoped to save by its program, included in the Water Plan, to "mechanically eradicate and control dense growths of preatophytes now infesting ... the flood plain of the Colorado River"—which, translated, meant a program to uproot and destroy the willows and tamarisks which grace the banks of the lower Colorado. Two hundred thousand acre feet a year is almost enough water to supply the needs of a city the size of Detroit.

The reservoirs would further waste water by seepage through the Canyon walls, just as water escapes through the sides of a leaky tub. How much this loss would be it was impossible to estimate—the Bureau's reports gave no figures for seepage, indeed they gave no evidence that the problem was even considered. The loss might be slight from Bridge Canyon reservoir, much of which would be contained within the impermeable schist. But it could be considerable in Marble Gorge, where the innumerable anostomotic tubes which pockmark the Redwall would tend to drain the water toward the east and recharge the groundwater table in the Navajo Reservation and New Mexico. No doubt this would be appreciated by the Navajos and New Mexicans, but this diversion of the Colorado was not part of the Plan.

Then again, there would be the millions of acre feet of water permanently sequestered in dead storage. Glen Canyon Dam, for instance, must impound 6,100,000 acre feet before it could generate one kilowatt of electricity. These 6,100,000 acre feet would run no turbines, water no fields, supply no towns with drinking water. Their sole purpose would be to raise the level of the lake to the point where additional water flowing into the reservoir would pass into the intake conduits at the dam. Between them, Marble Gorge and Bridge Canyon dams would hoard another 4,073,000 acre feet in dead storage. Together with Lake Powell, they would permanently store away, like money in a mattress, almost a year's average flow of the Colorado River—a year's flow of water, which, allowed to run down to Lake Mead, could not only generate power at Hoover Dam but could subsequently be used for irrigation or diverted to municipal water supply systems.

All this was bad enough, but the loss of water through evaporation would have a further serious effect. The water stored in reservoirs is not pure rain water, but contains tons of dissolved salts—bicarbonates, chlorides and sulfates of sodium, calcium and magnesium. Evaporation removes part of the water, but leaves the dissolved solids behind. And as a result, the concentration of salts increases. The salinity of Colorado River water has already become a severe problem. Tests of the water at Hoover Dam in 1956–57 showed a total of dissolved solids of 791 parts per million—compared with a nominal 500 ppm upper limit for acceptable drinking water.

Additional evaporation below Hoover Dam—from Lakes Mojave and Havasu and from the river itself—and the saline wastes dumped into the river from the reclamation project in the Wellton-Mohawk Valley in Arizona, have further impaired the quality of the water to such a point that, when it reaches Mexico, it is practically brine. In the winter of 1961 the salt content reached 2,700 ppm at the border, and the Mexicans, rather than use the water, let it run down to the Gulf of California. Crop losses were claimed on more than 100,000 acres, and the Mexican Government accused the United States Government of violating the 1944 treaty. To this, the State Department replied that although the treaty guaranteed Mexico 1,500,000 acre feet of water a year, it included no guarantee that the water would be usable. Subsequently, the United States changed its attitude and, in effect, acknowledged responsibility by joining the Mexican Government in efforts to find ways of averting further damage. But by 1964 nothing concrete had been done; ninety thousand acres in Baja California had been ruined for cultivation; and farmers south of the border were staging mass protest demonstrations which, according to the New York Times, were in danger of being taken over by leftists intent on precipitating violent border incidents.

Marble Gorge and Bridge Canyon dams, far from conserving water, would waste water in a region where every drop is precious, and would help adulterate the quality of the water that remained.

Perhaps the dams would serve to regulate the flow of the river?

Again, no.

River regulation is accomplished by providing long-term hold-over storage capacity which captures a river's excess flow during years of heavy run-off and releases water during dry years, thereby smoothing out the flow of the river. In 1959, the U.S. Geological Survey published two papers dealing with regulation of the Colorado River. In Circular 409, *Water Yield and Reservoir Storage in the United States*, Walter B. Langbein wrote: "Although in the East a considerable increase in usable water supply can be obtained by additional reservoir storage, some drainage basins in the West may already be approaching the limit. For example, the capacity of existing reservoirs in the Colorado River basin is nearly 35 million acre-feet. Most of this capacity, which is in Lake Mead, is used to regulate the flow of the main stem. The regulatory capacity soon will be nearly doubled by the construction of Glen Canyon Reservoir, which will have a usable capacity of about 20 million acre-feet. But evaporation imposes a ceiling on potential river regulation in an arid climate. . . . There is no significant gain in net regulation between 29 and 78 million acre-feet of capacity. The gain in regulation to be achieved by increasing the present 29 million acre-feet to nearly 50 million acre-feet of capacity appears to be largely offset by a corresponding increase in evaporation. . . . The Colorado River basin is an example of a river basin where storage development may be approaching, if not exceeding, the useful limit."

In Circular 410, *Probability Analysis Applied to a Water-Supply Problem*, Luna B. Leopold reached the same conclusion: "Total reservoir capacity in excess of about 40,000,000 acre-feet would achieve practically no additional water regulation if evaporation loss is subtracted from annual regulation." Amusingly enough the Colorado legislature, fearing that the U.S.G.S. circulars might jeopardize construction of more dams in the Upper Basin, financed a study of the papers by their own group of experts. The results of the study were published in 1961 (*Past and Probable Future Variations in Stream Flow in the Upper Colorado River*). And, to the chagrin of the legislators, they vindicated the U.S.G.S. circulars.

But the Department of the Interior, apparently anxious not to embarrass the Bureau of Reclamation, did not release the circulars until *after* Congress had approved Glen Canyon Dam. And thus, despite the fact that Hoover Dam alone was quite able to regulate the Colorado River (only once since the dam was finished had Lake Mead approached its 29 million acre-feet capacity), a colossal duplicate "regulating" facility was installed upstream where it regulates nothing but the river's flow through the Grand Canyon. And still unsatisfied, the Bureau had plans for an ultimate storage capacity on the Colorado of nearly 80 million acre-feet.

No, on an already over-regulated river, Marble Gorge and Bridge Canyon dams were not needed for regulation.

Would the proposed dams store water for irrigation purposes?

No. There would be no diversions of irrigation water from Marble and Bridge reservoirs.

If the dams would not conserve water, would not regulate the river's flow, would not store water for irrigation, what would they do?

They would produce power, period. With a combined peak capacity of 2.1 million kilowatts, they would generate an estimated 7.67 billion kilowatt-hours annually, the greater part of which would be sold to finance the various projects included in the Pacific Southwest Water Plan—including the dams themselves—and the remainder of which would be used to pump 1.2 million acre feet a year from Parker Dam, downstream from Hoover, into central Arizona. The total construction cost of the Plan was estimated at $3,126,000,000. Of this sum, $1,704,000,000 would go into projects proposed for immediate construction, the principal ones being Bridge Canyon Project ($511 million), Marble Gorge Project ($239 million), the California Aqueduct Enlargement to bring 1.2 million acre feet of water from northern to southern California ($240 million), and the Central Arizona Project ($527 million). A second stage, requiring further study, would cost $1,422,000,000, and would capture an additional 1.2 million acre feet of water from dams and reservoirs to be constructed, with unstudied destruction of scenery and native habitat, on northern California coastal streams such as the Trinity, Eel, Van Duzen, and Mad, and transport it through an elaborate system of conduits to the south for distribution to Arizona and southern California.

The core of the Plan was the Central Arizona Project. Without it, there would be no present need for the importation of the 1.2 million acre feet of water to southern California, since the importation was intended only to replace Colorado River water hitherto used by southern California but now to be diverted to the CAP. Nor would there be any alleged need for the Bridge Canyon and Marble Gorge dams.

Though Arizona had sought congressional authorization for the CAP for over a decade, no progress could be made toward implementation of the project until Glen Canyon Dam was completed to save Bridge and Marble dams from quick silting up, and until the conflicting claims of California and Arizona to Colorado River water were settled. In 1952, Arizona filed action in the United States Supreme Court, seeking a judicial determination of the two states' respective rights to water from the river. While the case was being argued, prudence might have dictated that southern California and Arizona tailor their development to their dependable supplies of water, which in Arizona's case amounted to about 1 million acre feet from the Colorado, another 1 million acre feet from Arizona surface streams (the Salt, Verde, Gila, Agua Fria, San Pedro and Santa Cruz rivers), and 1,250,000 acre feet which could safely be pumped from the underground water table. But southern California blithely accelerated its development as if the amount of water it was yearly drawing from the Colorado had been adjudicated to it in perpetuity. And, despite the fact that the Supreme Court could well have decided, in conformity with basic western water law, that since California had established prior use to the lion's share of

Colorado River water it was entitled to keep it, Arizona went for broke.

It welcomed and encouraged an explosive population and economic boom during the 1950's and early 1960's. Lands developed for irrigation jumped to 1.2 million acres—much of it in cotton which only served to swell the Nation's already burdensome cotton surplus. And it accomplished all this by overdrawing its groundwater account at a rate which by 1963 reached 2.2 million acre-feet a year. This, of course, could not go on forever. The water table was dropping fast, and pumping costs rising accordingly. The state was headed for water bankruptcy, and still it indulged in its headlong development. Arizonans, obviously, expected to be bailed out. And they proved to be right—in part, at least.

In June, 1963, the Supreme Court announced its decision in Arizona v. California, et al. Henceforth, California would be entitled to 4.4 million acre feet of the 7.5 million a year allowed the Lower Basin states under the Colorado River Compact. Arizona could appropriate 2.8 million acre feet. Nevada would have use of the balance of 300,000 acre feet. The Bureau of Reclamation moved fast. Five months before the Court's judgment, it released its first report on the Pacific Southwest Water Plan. In August, views and recommendations were solicited from the affected states and Federal agencies, and a second report, modified to incorporate these recommendations and to meet certain objections, was issued in January, 1964.

What would the Water Plan mean to Arizona? It would enable the state to draw 1.2 million acre feet of the 1.8 million which the Supreme Court had awarded it over and above the 1 million acre feet it already was using from the river. But since Arizona was overdrawing its groundwater reserves by 2.2 million acre feet a year, it was still left with a net deficit, if no further population and economic expansion took place, of 1 million acre feet. This deficit might perhaps be made up if the state took stringent measures on the watershed to increase yield from rainfall, improved farm-irrigation practices, made more careful use of municipal supplies, reused sewage effluent, completely lined canal systems, undertook desalinization and use of brackish waters in various sections of the state—and were satisfied with maintaining the present level of population and economic activity. But Arizonans in positions of influence and power were just as hypnotized by the fool's gold of Growth as their fellows across the Colorado in southern California. And there was every reason to expect that they would use the additional Colorado River water, *and* continue to

pump their groundwater—the Bureau had no plans
top this—until another Federal plan were devised
il them out again.

hat form would such growth take? It would not be
ultural—no new lands, it was emphasized by the
au, were to be brought under irrigation by the
fic Southwest Water Plan. In both Arizona and
fornia, the trend was toward continued encroach-
t on irrigated and irrigable lands by industrial and
mercial enterprises and by subdivisions. And the
fic Southwest Water Plan's principal effect would be
cilitate continued urbanization of the region. This
t be thought good or bad, depending on one's atti-
, But this was not reclamation. And by appropriating
self the planning, construction and management of
ects included in the Plan, the Bureau of Reclamation
greatly exceeding the limits of its proper functions.
gressman John P. Saylor of Pennsylvania, ranking
ublican member of the House Committee on Inte-
and Insular Affairs, had protested this tendency on
part of the Bureau: "The Federal reclamation pro-
," he said, "was begun over half a century ago for
asic purpose of reclaiming the arid, barren lands of
West in order to make them more productive. In the
ing decades, and particularly in the past few years,
policies and programs of the bureaucrats in the
au of Reclamation have wandered so far afield from
basic goal that it seems reclamation has become of
incidental importance. The present officials of the
au of Reclamation have become so preoccupied with
npts to develop unnecessary hydroelectric power
ects and Federal power transmission grids that their
king has become as arid and barren as the western
s they were formerly charged with reclaiming."
Saylor warned that this might lead to honest recla-
on programs falling into disrepute with members of
gress and other influential groups. He added, "one of
olleagues from the eastern part of the United States
ested the Bureau of Reclamation change its name to
Bureau of Federal Power. For this reason I repeat,
amation program is needed to reclaim the Bureau of
amation for its original purpose before it is too
"

he Bureau contended that Bridge Canyon and
ble Gorge dams were essential to produce revenues
nance the construction of the Water Plan's water
sion projects. But since the Water Plan was *not* a
mation project, Bridge Canyon dam at least was
ly illegal. Its reservoir would invade Grand Canyon
onal Park and Monument despite the fact that the
law clearly stated that such invasion would be counte-
nanced only "when necessary for the development and
maintenance of government reclamation projects."

The dams would be wasteful of water, injurious to its
quality, unneeded for river regulation, destructive of
some of the most magnificent scenery on the face of this
planet, and Bridge Canyon dam would cause a serious,
illegal and precedent-setting infringement of the National
Park and Monument System. And to compound the
outrage, neither Bridge Canyon nor Marble Gorge Dam
was necessary: the power and resultant revenues which
they would produce could be obtained by other means
in *much* less time and at *much* less cost.

Of course this would not become apparent by reading
only the Bureau's reports. For the Bureau has made public no comparisons of the costs of the proposed dams
with those of alternative power plants. Such an evalua-
tion would appear to be essential when presenting the
case for dams whose only raison d'être is power production. But the Bureau has failed to publish comparative
figures because to do so might be fatal to its future plans.

Including the dams to be built on the Paria and Little
Colorado rivers to protect the mainstream dams from
silting up within a century, the Bridge Canyon and
Marble Gorge dam projects would cost a total of $750
million. Steam plants generating the same peak capacity
as the dams would cost, to use a conservative figure,
about $125 per kilowatt, or about $263 million. This
would be only 35 per cent of the investment cost for the
hydroelectric plants, representing a saving on initial cost
of $487 million, *or almost the price of Bridge Canyon Dam!*

Bridge Canyon and Marble Gorge dams would market
their power at 6 mills per kilowatt hour. But a published
analysis by professional engineer Alexander Hildebrand
has shown that steam plants, if given the same tax and
interest benefits that are being granted the Bureau's
hydroelectric plants, could sell electricity for less than
5 mills per kilowatt hour. The Bureau's 6 mills price is
an artificial one which does not reflect—and will not
recover—the real costs of the dam projects to the taxpayer. The 3 per cent interest rate charged to the Pacific
Southwest Water Plan projects is less than the cost of the
money to the Government. (Long-term Government
bonds currently bear an interest rate of more than 4 per
cent, and the American Society of Civil Engineers has
suggested that Federally-financed hydroelectric developments should return a rate of at least 4.5 per cent.

Both natural causes and technological developments
would contribute to the rapid obsolescence of the dams.
Hydropower is usually thought of as an indefinitely re-

newable resource, but it lacks this advantage on the silt-laden Colorado. Within a relatively short time (200, 300, 400 years?—the exact period is difficult to estimate) the reservoirs would be silted in, a process accelerated by the undermining and spalling of the Canyon walls such as is already occurring in Glen Canyon. Why build dams with a useful life expectancy of a few centuries in an area with coal reserves sufficient to generate equivalent power at the same rate for thousands of years?

Technological progress, on the other hand, could make the dams obsolete long before there were any appreciable silting in of the reservoirs, and could undermine the rickety financial structure of the Pacific Southwest Water Plan. In working out the pay-out schedule for the Plan, the Bureau assumed that its 6 mills price for peaking power would still be attractive in the year 2047, the year to which the payout study extends. In effect the Bureau gambled that power costs would remain static over this period, in spite of all the evidence to the contrary. Not only have steam plants burning conventional fossil fuels become increasingly efficient over the years, but the day may be near when atomic energy will begin to produce really inexpensive electricity. Some scientists are even predicting a technological breakthrough with the hydrogen-fusion process—the ultimate in energy production since it is the very source of solar energy—perhaps by the end of the century, or before the Bureau's construction program's first stage is thirty years old. Such a breakthrough would not only make the dams obsolete as a source of power, but would make possible the economical desalting of sea water and thereby obviate the need for complicated, astronomically expensive and scenery-damaging transfers of water from one watershed, say northern California, to another.

Richard C. Bradley, Associate Professor of Physics at Colorado College, wrote in *Pacific Discovery*, journal of the California Academy of Sciences: "Regardless of whether or not nuclear energy ever becomes a practical reality, hydropower is destined for ever *decreasing* importance in the United States. It is well known that if every bit of usable stream in the country were developed to its full capacity, the total hydropower generated would furnish only about 5% of our total energy requirements, and these are expected to double in twenty years."

Even the Bureau recognizes this in its report on the Water Plan: "Installed hydroelectric capacity will continue to increase," it states, "but its relative magnitude will be dwarfed by the increase in thermal generation capacity." And farther on: "The total proposed Bridge Canyon and Marble [Gorge] hydroelectric capacity will

provide only a small increment of the projected fut[ure] power demand of the area. . ." But the Bureau then f[alls] back on the last ditch argument that hydropower can [be] turned on and off at will and thus can meet peak po[wer] requirements "more economically and with greater fl[exi]bility than thermal generating units."

In August, 1963, during Senate subcommittee heari[ngs] on the Central Arizona Project, the following excha[nge] took place between Senator Clinton P. Anderson of N[ew] Mexico and Reclamation Commissioner Floyd Domi[ny.]

Senator Anderson commented: "On August 14 [the] Federal Power Commission released a National Po[wer] Survey Advisory Committee report forecasting a ma[jor] role for nuclear powerplants meeting electric ene[rgy] needs of California beginning in the 1970's. You can[not] get [Bridge Canyon Dam] finished until 10 years. So t[hat] runs to the 1970's."

Mr. Dominy replied: "That is fine. I do not c[are] whether we have thermal power by atomic energy, [by] coal, by whatever heat source that uses up energy [in] creating the steam—hydropower will still fit into [it] masterfully as peaking power . . . How dramatic thi[s] was driven home to me not long ago when I was a[t a] powerplant when the noon hour was reached. The op[er]ator just pulled the switch and cut the generating units for an hour to save water—because the factory s[hut] down, and the peak use was closed out for one ho[ur.] And to save an hour's water, they cut the two gen[er]ators and turbines off, and then an hour later threw [the] switch back on. You cannot do that with steam."

Surely the American public is being asked to cond[one] the permanent defacement of much of the Grand Cany[on] and the precedent-setting invasion of Grand Cany[on] National Park for weightier reasons than the alle[ged] greater flexibility of hydropower and the convenience [of] turning it on and off by the flick of a switch? To be su[re,] the report also claims that hydropower can meet p[eak] requirements more economically. But that is a [bald] statement unsupported by any comparative figures. H[ow] much more economically, one would like to know? H[ow] much more—or less—economically than pump stora[ge?] Than new thermal plants designed especially for peak[ing] power? What of nuclear power, of which it has b[een] claimed that it peaks as nicely as hydro? What would [a] peaking comparison be once a major intertie has b[een] completed and power can be switched as the need ar[ises] throughout the Intermountain and Far West?

Even assuming that hydropower holds and contin[ues] to hold a small price advantage over thermal power [in] supplying short-term peak power requirements—in v[iew] of the minor part which electricity from the dams is expected to play in meeting the future power demand of the Southwest, by what fractional per cent would the area's power bill be increased if its needs for peaking power were met wholly by steam plants? Would this fractional bit justify the immensely greater initial expense of the dams, the waste of precious water from the reservoirs—and the irreparable damage to the Grand Canyon? Are the citizens of the whole nation prepared to subsidize the growth of the Southwest to that extent?

These are all questions which the Bureau's reports do not raise, let alone answer. These are questions which were not raised during the Senate hearings on the Central Arizona Project, let alone answered. But that is not surprising, since the expert witnesses were all from the Bureau, and since the attitude of the majority of the Senate subcommittee members seemed to corroborate John Graves' dictum, in his delightful *Goodbye to a River:* "When some one official dreams up a dam, it generally goes in. Dams are ipso facto good all by themselves, like mothers and flags."

Bradley in his article posed another logical question: "How does the Bureau get away with this? How did it acquire the license to wreck the most magnificent of our western canyons with reservoirs so manifestly wasteful and superfluous?

"The answer is simple. The technical flaws in the Bureau's plan were never seriously considered by Congress [during hearings on Glen Canyon Dam]. The Hildebrand report on power was virtually ignored, and the Geological Survey reports on river regulation were not released by the Interior Department until *after* the project had been authorized. At the Congressional hearings Geological Survey witnesses (and also National Park Service witnesses) were conspicuous by their absence. All of the experts came from the Bureau of Reclamation and they were not about to advertise that their project was wasteful and superfluous."

Bradley described the operation of "a vicious circle which is very difficult to break into. A large Federal bureau draws up a plan for a huge public works project. It is huge because the bureau needs to justify the existence of its own very large organization. Being huge, the project naturally attracts the interest and enthusiastic support of the local chambers of commerce as no smaller project ever could. Strong business support inevitably means strong political support. By the time the proposal reaches Congress, with all the momentum of an express train, it is already too late to discuss its merits and defects objectively . . . So, even though it is riddled with flaws, it becomes law, the large Federal bureau becomes still larger, and the wheel starts around again."

It is interesting to note, in this regard, that Arizona Senator Barry Goldwater, who had opposed many projects for the development of natural resources that involved the use of Federal funds, and who had proposed that the Government dispose of its holdings in the Tennessee Valley Authority, co-authored the Central Arizona Project bill with Senator Carl Hayden. Yet neither Senator is now doing his state a favor. There is a chance that so long as the Central Arizona Project is designed so as to require the destruction of the integrity of the Grand Canyon, conservationist sentiment throughout the country will be strong enough to block its approval by Congress. Even if Congress did approve the Water Plan, with its C.A.P. feature, ten years would pass during which Arizona would have to make do with its present water supply, before Bridge Canyon and Marble Gorge dams could begin generating power to pump Colorado River water into central Arizona. The water could be delivered far sooner if thermal plants were built to supply the power. And the saving on initial cost earned by building steam plants instead of the dams would be more than sufficient to develop enough power, and to build aqueducts large enough, to deliver Arizona's full 1,800,000 acre feet of Colorado River water instead of 1,200,000—all that the Water Plan can promise.

If present laws do not permit the Bureau to subsidize water diversion projects by the sale of other than hydroelectric power, then for the sake of common sense, economics, and the preservation of the Grand Canyon's unspoiled majesty, let Congress change the laws. What is inflexible is not thermal power, much as the Bureau would have us think, but rather the failure or refusal by the Bureau and other public officials to consider alternatives to the big dam concept. If Bridge Canyon and Marble Gorge dams were built, and then within a generation proved to be obsolete, it would be too late to save the Grand Canyon. The damage would be irrevocable. And for eons to come Bridge Canyon Dam, Marble Gorge Dam, and Glen Canyon Dam would stand athwart the Colorado River, their reservoirs silted in, their turbines dead, and their concrete parabolas surviving as monuments to the inflexibility of man.

12. Epilogue

Had OUR Colorado River trip been a well plotted drama, it would have ended at Separation Canyon. In the seventeen days and 240 miles from our departure at Lee's Ferry, all the subthemes of the Grand Canyon story had been presented to us: its geology, its natural history, its impact on man, and man's impact, past, present and future, on it. We had come to know the Canyon and the river in their varied moods—friendly or hostile (as it seemed to me) according to the state of the weather, challenging or welcoming (again as it seemed to me) according to whether the water was fast or slow. The Secretary of the Interior, like a *deus ex machina*, had contributed added tension in the last act of the drama by shutting off the water at Glen Canyon Dam, but we had conquered this challenge too by reaching Separation Canyon ahead of the low water.

Still, geography dictated that we had another forty miles to go before we were out of the Grand Canyon, and five miles on top of that before we would meet the boats which would tow us to Temple Bar over the sapphire waters of Lake Mead. So our trip lasted another two days, although they were somewhat anticlimactic. There were no more rapids to add spice to the rowing. The inner Canyon tended to widen as we neared its lower end, and increasingly the river ran between great silt flats that had been deposited by Lake Mead when it was high. The surface of the flats was sometimes bare and cracked by the heat of the sun; sometimes it was covered with a jungle of tamarisks. A line on the Canyon walls, like a ring of dirt in a bathtub, clearly marked the level which Lake Mead once had reached. Were the walls of Marble Gorge, and of Lower Granite Gorge above Bridge Canyon Dam, to be similarly defaced? Were the river's shores between the mouths of Havasu and Kanab creeks, or in the neighborhood of Lee's Ferry, destined to resemble the shores near Pierce Ferry, desolate wastes of stinking silt fields?

We emerged from the Grand Canyon before noon on the nineteenth day of our voyage. As I looked back at the imposing façade of the Grand Wash Cliffs, the western frontier of the Grand Canyon country, I realized with pride and gratitude that I had become a Canyoneer—pride at joining the small but growing club of perhaps 900 souls that had been founded by Major Powell and his party, gratitude for the circumstances that had made it possible for me to enjoy one of the greatest experiences still available in this world of increasingly standardized mass recreation.

But there was a sadness mixed in with my feelings. How many more Americans would have the chance that I had had? How many more would know the elation we had felt, living for three weeks in the midst of the world's grandest scenery, independent and self-reliant, intimate with the natural world from which we all had sprung, freed for a period from the impositions of civilized life with its grave or petty problems? How many would know the peace of drifting along with the river, the only sounds being the creaking of an oarlock, the slurping of the water against the oarblades, or perhaps the song of a wren seeming to tumble down the Canyon walls? How many would know the quickening of the spirit that comes when the boat glides down the tongue of a rapid, and dances exuberantly among the leaping waves? Or the joys of an evening campfire, when the body is agreeably tired and the spirit relaxed, the breeze spreads the scent of the burning driftwood and the fire's glow flickers against the Canyon wall? How many would know the satisfaction that comes even from enduring the discomfort of a Canyon storm and seeing themselves, as Stegner put it, "single, separate, vertical and individual in the world, part of the environment of trees and rocks and soil, brother to the other animals, part of the natural world and competent to belong in it"?

Not many, if the Bureau of Reclamation succeeded in its plans. Of the Colorado River's 280 miles through the Grand Canyon, just over one third, or 104 miles, would remain a flowing river. And even this remnant would be inaccessible to boatmen, since there is no place between the Marble Gorge dam site and Kanab Creek, where the Bridge Canyon reservoir would begin, to which one could bring a boat down to the river. Yes, there would be boating recreation on the two reservoirs—but recreation of a type which is available on a hundred other man-made lakes throughout the country. Water skiers and bathing beauties have their rights, of course. But they also have their place—and that is not the Grand Canyon.

There is no gorge in the world quite like the Grand Canyon. There is no river in the country quite like the virile Colorado. The flowing river is both the heart and the main artery of the Canyon. Destroy the living river and the Grand Canyon itself would in a sense die. For the river is the life force of the Canyon, the chief architect of its carving, the continuing thread which gives meaning to this whole vast, incomparable wonder of nature. No amount of man-days of recreation on the Bridge Canyon or Marble Gorge reservoirs would compensate for the destruction of the wholeness of the Canyon. The entire American people—even those who would never dream of braving the Colorado's rapids—the entire world for that matter, would be the losers. For you cannot impair one of the world's greatest marvels without infringing the birthright of every man.

Nor would the damage end with the "peripheral invasion," as Secretary Udall termed it, of Grand Canyon National Park. Make no mistake about it: if Grand Canyon National Park is invaded by the reservoir, Dinosaur National Monument will be the next to go. One of the most telling arguments adduced by conservationists in their successful fight against Echo Park and Split Mountain dams had been that such infringements of Dinosaur's integrity would set a precedent for later infringements of other units of the National Park and Monument System. The conservationists won then—but if the Grand Canyon is not considered too sacred for such uses certainly Dinosaur will not be. And what then would stand in the way of other water and power developments by the Bureau of Reclamation or Army Corps of Engineers that would adversely affect Glacier National Park (the Glacier View dam, Belly River and Waterton Lake diversions), Yellowstone National Park (a dam on Yellowstone Lake, the Bechler Basin project), Grand Teton National Park (Buffalo River dam), Yosemite National Park (the Wawona project), Kings Canyon National Park (dams proposed at Cedar Grove, Tehipite Valley, Paradise Valley, Sentinel, Simpson Meadow, not to mention fifteen power and storage structures in Kings River High Sierra), Mammoth Caves National Park (Mining City dam), Big Bend National Park (dams proposed on the Rio Grande within the park), or Arches National Monument (the Moab dam, in the Bureau's inventory). Like circus barkers, the bureaus would tout the recreation benefits to accrue from these projects. But of course the recreation gambit is only a public relations trick. The basic purpose of the proposed Marble Gorge and Bridge Canyon dams is not to create recreation opportunities. It is not even to develop electric power—

since alternate sources of power exist which would not require the desecration of one of the wonders of the world. It is merely to justify the big Bureau's continued existence. For, as Bradley put it, "a dam building bureau must keep moving if it is to survive. When it has finished one project it must find another, and then another, and another, and so on until every river is saturated with dams."

Arizona has a water problem. That fact is inescapable. But the damming of the Grand Canyon is only one possible solution to this problem—and an incomplete and fearfully expensive one at that. If the state is to grow from its present population of 1.5 million people to nearly 10 million by the year 2020, as the experts predict, all the water in the Colorado will not suffice for its needs. Plans are already on the drawing boards to divert water from the Snake River into the Colorado, or to import Columbia River water. A proposal has even been made to transport water to the Pacific Southwest all the way from the Yukon, at a total cost that would equal a sizable part of the national debt.

And thus the growth of one area of the country has repercussions that reach ever farther from its borders. After a while, one begins to wonder about the sense of it all. Would Arizona be a better place to live in with six times its present population? Must Phoenix become another Los Angeles? Is the transfer of huge quantities of water to permit the artificial development of arid lands the most economic use of our national resources? Would the money invested in such prodigious water works not return greater benefits if it were invested elsewhere?

I suppose if we accept as a national policy that every resource of the country must be developed to the limit to support the greatest possible human population, then we should right now give up the fight to save any untouched vestiges of our natural heritage. All rivers must be dammed, to prevent their wasting water into the ocean, and the consequent destruction of the beauty of natural rivers must be shrugged off as one of the prices of progress. By all means let us build Bridge Canyon and Marble Gorge dams—and the Kanab Creek Diversion Project as well, as an integral part of Reclamation's Master Plan. It does not matter that there is no present necessity for these projects: they are part of the maximum development of the Colorado River. You have to keep building, you have to keep growing, you have to keep moving ahead, the developers insist, or the economy will stagnate. The developers cannot envisage such a thing as a prosperous and yet stable economy. The economy is either vigorous and expanding, or it is sick and stagnant.

I, for one, cannot accept this postulate. If we assume that the free enterprise system can only prosper through continuous expansion primed by population growth, then we must agree with the Marxists that it carries within it the seeds of its own dissolution. For the more crowded the nation becomes, the more stringent will Government controls necessarily be.

Yet to question the assumption that the population explosion is inevitable and desirable "is possibly the greatest heresy of all," Secretary Udall told the 1962 Wilderness Conference in San Francisco. "Government planners, if I am to judge by what comes across my desk, operate in a sort of bureaucratic trance when it comes to projections which indicate that the U.S. population will almost double in forty years. And it seems to be a corollary of this assumption that the good, the true, and the beautiful will go hand in hand with a more populous nation. Is it not time that we seriously question the bases of these assumptions?

"Is it not time to give serious consideration to the 'ecology of man'—the relation of human population to its environment? Is it not time to ask whether man, as part of nature, is subject to the laws that govern other species, particularly the law that for every species in a particular environment there is an optimum population?

"... Biologists find that for some species, as the amount of living space decreases beyond a certain point, neurotic strains are set up in the individual and his higher faculties atrophy.

"How does this apply to humans? What is the proper man-land ratio? How much 'living space' do humans need for the best functioning? These are questions that are almost wholly ignored, but that are vital to our future."

Later in his talk, the Secretary discussed the impact of an indefinitely expanding population on our parks and wilderness areas. "Even assuming that some parcels of wilderness can be held against the pressures of increasing numbers of people, the only way of preserving them would be to do what we do with any commodity in short supply—ration it ... You would make reservations and wait your turn, it would be as simple as that ... Park and wilderness rationing in this country is not merely a prospect for the remote future but could conceivably become necessary in the years or decades immediately ahead. To get in the car when the mood strikes you and find natural sanctuary from the pressures of modern life—as we do at present—may become a privilege to look back on, in the years to come, as we customarily look back on 'golden ages' of the past."

It is rather ironic that Secretary Udall, who so eloquently warned of the perils of growth, should be prepared to sacrifice the Grand Canyon to such growth. And it is tragic when one considers that the sacrifice is unnecessary. There are other ways of producing the power to pump Colorado River water into central Arizona. There are any number of other ways of financing the Central Arizona Project, and the delivery of replacement water to southern California. Only the inflexibility of our Government leaders and the self-interest of the Bureau of Reclamation have caused the alternatives to be ignored. Our self-interest as civilized human beings demands that these alternatives be explored and implemented, and that the Grand Canyon be preserved intact as time and the flowing river have fashioned it. Our self-interest demands that Grand Canyon National Park be expanded from its present illogical and incomplete kernel to include the whole of the geographical Grand Canyon, from the Vermilion Cliffs to the Grand Wash Cliffs, and that the basic law establishing the Park be amended specifically to forbid the construction of dams or other similar works within the confines of the Canyon.

This would be a project to challenge the imagination of the American people. Indeed it would be a fitting monument to the character of a people which, alone of the major nations of the world, has had the foresight to preserve a major part of its natural heritage. To paraphrase Newton B. Drury, fourth Director of the National Park Service, America is not so poor that it needs to sacrifice its magnificent places for power generation, nor so rich in such places that it can afford to.

The next time you visit the Grand Canyon, you might find yourself a quiet perch somewhere on the rim. Look off through the blue cast of space at the cliffs and terraces and amphitheaters and temples, search out the thin thread of the Colorado, rumbling through the gorge it has cut into the antiquity of the world, and breathe in your part of it all. It is within your power—and of those you can awaken—to make certain that this will endure. In a special way, Edwin Arlington Robinson's admonition in *Tristram* applies to the creative genius in every man:

> *... you are one*
> *Of the time-sifted few that leave the world,*
> *When they are gone, not the same place it was.*
> *Mark what you leave.*

The Idea of Wilderness

We saw ourselves as indeed a part of the wildness of the universe. That is
our nature. Our noblest, happiest character develops with the influence of
wilderness. Away from it we tend to degenerate into the squalor of slums or
the frustration of clinical couches. With the wilderness we are at home.

Some of us think we see this so clearly that for ourselves, for our children,
our continuing posterity, and our fellow man we covet with a consuming
intensity the fullness of the human development that keeps its contact with
wildness. Out of the wilderness has come the substance of our culture, and
with a living wilderness—it is our faith—we shall have also a vibrant, vital
culture, an enduring civilization of healthful happy people who like Antaeus
perpetually renew themselves in contact with the earth. . . . We are engaged
in an effort that may well be expected to continue until its right consumma-
tion, by our successors if need be. Working to preserve in perpetuity is a
great inspiration. We are not fighting a rear-guard action, we are facing a
frontier. We are not slowing down a force that inevitably will destroy all the
wilderness there is. We are generating another force, never to be wholly
spent, that, renewed generation after generation, will be always effective in
preserving wilderness. We are not fighting progress. We are making it.

We are not dealing with a vanishing wilderness. We are working for a
wilderness forever.

HOWARD ZAHNISER

To Albert Schweitzer, who said, "Man has lost the capacity to foresee and to forestall. He will end by destroying the earth."

RACHEL CARSON
(*Silent Spring* dedication)

Yet the coming of man was quiet enough. Even after he arrived, even after his strange retarded youth had given him the brain which opened up to him the dimensions of time and space, he walked softly. If, as was true, he had sloughed instinct away for a new interior world of consciousness, he did something which at the same time revealed his continued need for the stability which had preserved his ancestors. Scarcely had he stepped across the border of the old instinctive world when he began to create the world of custom. He was using reason, his new attribute, to remake, in another fashion, a substitute for the lost instinctive world of nature. . . .

There is a story about one of our great atomic physicists—a story for whose authenticity I cannot vouch, and therefore I will not mention his name. I hope, however, with all my heart that it is true. If it is not, then it ought to be, for it illustrates well what I mean by a growing self-awareness, a sense of responsibility about the universe.

This man, one of the chief architects of the atomic bomb, so the story runs, was out wandering in the woods one day with a friend when he came upon a small tortoise. Overcome with pleasurable excitement, he took up the tortoise and started home, thinking to surprise his children with it. After a few steps he paused and surveyed the tortoise doubtfully.

"What's the matter?" asked his friend.

Without responding, the great scientist slowly retraced his steps as precisely as possible, and gently set the turtle down upon the exact spot from which he had taken him up.

Then he turned solemnly to his friend. "It just struck me," he said, "that perhaps, for one man, I have tampered enough with the universe." He turned, and left the turtle to wander on its way.

The man who made that remark was one of the best of the modern men, and what he had devised had gone down into the whirlpool. "I have tampered enough," he said. It was not a denial of science. It was a final recognition that . . . science is not enough for man. It is not the road back to the waiting Garden, for that road lies through the heart of man. Only when man has recognized this fact will science become what it was for Bacon, something to speak of as "touching upon Hope." Only then will man be truly human.

LOREN EISELEY

CLYDE THOMAS: *Evening, below Toroweap, Mile 177*

Science contributes moral as well as material blessings to the world. Its great moral contribution is objectivity, or the scientific point of view. This means doubting everything except facts; it means hewing to the facts, let the chips fall where they may. One of the facts hewn to by science is that every river needs more people, and all people need more inventions, and hence more science; the good life depends on the indefinite extension of this chain of logic. That the good life on any river may likewise depend on the perception of its music, and the preservation of some music to perceive, is a form of doubt not yet entertained by science.

ALDO LEOPOLD

The "control of nature" is a phrase conceived in arrogance, born of the Neanderthal age of biology and philosophy, when it was supposed that nature exists for the convenience of man. The concepts and practices of applied entomology for the most part date from that Stone Age of science. It is our alarming misfortune that so primitive a science has armed itself with the most modern and terrible weapons, and that in turning them against the insects it has also turned them against the earth.

RACHEL CARSON

P HYDE: Deer Creek, Mile 136.3

I am pessimistic about the human race because it is too ingenious for its own good. Our approach to nature is to beat it into submission. We would stand a better chance of survival if we accommodated ourselves to this planet and viewed it appreciatively instead of skeptically and dictatorially.

E. B. WHITE

I am convinced that man has suffered in his separation from the soil and from the other living creatures of the world; the evolution of his intellect has outrun his needs as an animal, and as yet he must still, for security, look long at some portion of the earth as it was before he tampered with it.

GAVIN MAXWELL

Once in a lifetime, if one is lucky, one so merges with sunlight and air and running water that whole eons, the eons that mountains and deserts know, might pass in a single afternoon without discomfort. The mind has sunk away into its beginnings among old roots and the obscure tricklings and movings that stir inanimate things. . . . one can never quite define this secret; but it has something to do, I am sure, with common water. Its substance reaches everywhere; it touches the past and prepares the future; it moves under the poles and wanders thinly in the heights of air. It can assume forms of exquisite perfection in a snowflake, or strip the living to a single shining bone cast up by the sea.

LOREN EISELEY

PHILIP HYDE: Upper Deer Creek Falls

... Then someone found a shell embedded in rock on a mountain top; someone saw the birth of a new star in the inviolable Empyrean heavens, someone watched a little patch of soil carried by a stream into the valley. Another saw a forest buried under ancient clays and wondered. Some heretical idler observed a fish in stone. All these things had doubtless been seen many times before, but human interests were changing. . . .

Erosion was beginning to be faintly glimpsed as a power at work in nature. "That the height of the mountains doth continually diminish," muses John Ray, "is very likely." Our knowledge of time would have to be greatly altered before anyone would inquire whether persistent forces might be at work which would prevent the total denudation of the land and its eventual disappearance into the engulfing sea.

. . . It is with the coming of man that a vast hole seems to open in nature, a vast black whirlpool spinning faster and faster, consuming flesh, stones, soil, minerals, sucking down the lightning, wrenching power from the atom, until the ancient sounds of nature are drowned in the cacophony of something which is no longer nature, something instead which is loose and knocking at the world's heart, something demonic and no longer planned—escaped, it may be—spewed out of nature, contending in a final giant's game against its master.

LOREN EISELEY

PHILIP HYDE: In Ruby Canyon, Mile 104.6

Someday, I hope, I may see for myself the Apus shrimp (which isn't a shrimp) flourishing briefly in some pool which temporarily fills a depression in that Kaibab sandstone laid down at just about the time when the trilobite was making his last stand. I should like to see him clothed in the curious shell that looks old-fashioned even to the layman's eye and swimming on his back as the trilobites are believed to have done and as the young of the horseshoe crabs still do. It is the nearest any man can come to peering into a Paleozoic sea.

JOSEPH WOOD KRUTCH

The wisest, the most enlightened, the most remotely long-seeing exploitation of resources is not enough, for the simple reason that the whole concept of exploitation is so false and so limited that in the end it will defeat itself and the earth will have been plundered no matter how scientifically and farseeingly the plundering has been done.

Every day the science of ecology is making clearer the factual aspect as it demonstrates those more and more remote interdependencies which, no matter how remote they are, are crucial even for us.

JOSEPH WOOD KRUTCH

PHILIP HYDE: *Along Monument Creek, Mile 93.5*

Those who would cut the timber, slaughter the animals as game, turn cattle loose to graze, flood the area with dams, or even open them up to real estate subdivision are fond of saying, "After all, human needs come first." But of what needs and of what human beings are we thinking? Of the material needs (or rather profits) of a few ranchers and lumbermen, or of the mental and physical health, the education and spiritual experiences, of a whole population? We do not tear down a high school because the building industry can prove that it could profitably erect an apartment house on the site and that tenants would be glad to occupy it. We say, instead, that education pays off in a different way and that the space occupied by schools is not wasted. Much the same thing we say also of the space taken up by the green of a city square. But if parks and other public lands are to be held only until someone can show that a "use" has been found for them, they will not last very much longer. If we recognize that there is more than one kind of utility and that the parks are, at the present moment, being put to the best use to be found for them, then they may last a long time —until, perhaps, overpopulation has reached the point where the struggle for mere animal survival is so brutal that no school or theater, no concert hall or church, can be permitted to "waste" the land on which it stands.

JOSEPH WOOD KRUTCH

Men talk much of matter and energy, of the struggle for existence that molds the shape of life. These things exist, it is true; but more delicate, elusive, quicker than the fins in water, is that mysterious principle known as "organization," which leaves all other mysteries concerned with life stale and insignificant by comparison. . . . Like some dark and passing shadow within matter, it cups out the eyes' small windows or spaces the notes of a meadow lark's song in the interior of a mottled egg. That principle —I am beginning to suspect —was there before the living in the deeps of water.

The temperature has risen. The little stinging needles have given way to huge flakes floating in like white leaves blown from some great tree in open space. In the car, switching on the lights, I examine one intricate crystal on my sleeve before it melts. No utilitarian philosophy explains a snow crystal, no doctrine of use or disuse. Water has merely leapt out of vapor and thin nothingness in the night sky to array itself in form. There is no logical reason for the existence of a snowflake any more than there is for evolution. It is an apparition from that mysterious shadow world beyond nature, that final world which contains —if anything contains —the explanation of men and catfish and green leaves.

LOREN EISELEY

PHILIP HYDE: Desert Plume and mallow, Marble Gorge

Time and raindrops! It took enormous effort to discover the potentialities of both those forces. It took centuries before the faint trickling from cottage eaves and gutters caught the ear of some inquiring scholar. Men who could visualize readily the horrors of a universal Flood were deaf to the roar of the invisible Niagara falling into the rain barrel outside their window. They could not hear it because they lived in a time span so short that the only way geologic change could be effected was by the convulsions of earthquakes, or the forty torrential days and nights that brought the Biblical Deluge. . . .

LOREN EISELEY

For many of us the Biblical bush still burns, and there is a deep mystery in the heart of a simple seed. If I seem for a time to be telling the story of how man came under the domain of law, how he reluctantly gave up his dreams and found his own footsteps wandering backward until on some far hillside they were transmuted into the footprints of a beast, it is only that we may assess more clearly that strange world into which we have been born —we, compounded of dust, and the light of a star.

CLYDE THOMAS: *Upriver from Hopi Point, evening*

These are things which other nations can never recover. Should we lose them, we could not recover them either. The generation now living may very well be that which will make the irrevocable decision whether or not America will continue to be for centuries to come the one great nation which had the foresight to preserve an important part of its heritage. If we do not preserve it, then we shall have diminished by just that much the unique privilege of being an American.

JOSEPH WOOD KRUTCH

DAVID BROWER: Floor, Cathedral in the Desert

Remember These Things Lost

THE LAST DAYS OF GLEN CANYON

he approach to Music Temple was so beautiful that ple arrived there hushed. Photographers never quite ured what you saw. It was only a short walk from the est of float trips down a living river in Glen Canyon, thousands had seen it. Millions, in the generations to e, should have had a chance to stand by the quiet pool, ook up at the flutings where the waterfall entered, to out at the cliffs that echoed the music this place was ed for when Powell first found it. But the rising wa-of Lake Powell have already inundated everything that tered in the temple and have obliterated the matchless roach to its serenity.

n mid-June 1964 the approach to the Cathedral in the ert was still above the rising Lake Powell, but not far ve it. There were still twenty minutes to walk and fifty to climb. It was not easy to travel the distance without rence, or without being grateful that an already beau-l world could here exceed itself. Mysterious seepings erned the tapestries and living green tinged the sand-e's red. The trail was Clear Creek itself—a stream could make you look twice at the country it flowed ugh, at the colors it watered and revealed. Everywhere looked you knew what a setting meant to a place. And he Cathedral, whether you looked up at evening or in morning at this miracle of color and design, or whether looked at the gardens by the altar or the stream that ved from the nave, you knew what this place meant to etting. There would never be anything like it again.

he Bureau operating Glen Canyon dam will destroy place, too, and all that it meant or could mean through-this civilization's time. It will begin to go under just oon as the reservoir is allowed to rise a mere 25 feet ve the minimum level needed to produce power. A full rvoir would wipe out all trace of the great room. At water its bleached remnants would be exhumed. All

this will produce electricity at a reasonably competitive cost—electricity that could have come from coal for centuries, and from the atom after that, but is coming instead from the destruction of places like the Cathedral, which man could neither build nor restore. The engineers call this deprivation progress and speak of making accessible that which they put forever beyond man's reach.

Only a miracle could save Glen Canyon's Cathedral. Clear thinking, compounded with devotion to the things that make America beautiful and applied with conviction, can still save in Grand Canyon the only near equivalent to the Glen Canyon excellence that still exists on earth. Or apathy can let the Bureau of Reclamation win by default—and permanently deprive mankind of a piece of his environment that need not and should not be sacrificed. People—you, you and the people you confront from day to day who hear you—need to know. They will somehow need to act from their knowledge that it takes a living river to keep a canyon alive, including the Grand Canyon of the Colorado. Kept alive, this canyon is still more: it can remain a symbol of man's remembering not to be too arrogant about the natural forces that built him and that built the only earth he is equipped to survive on.

What follows is a reminder of the monumental loss to all world that compulsive engineering has brought about already in Glen Canyon, and will even have exceeded when late spring finds the Cathedral in the Desert gone.

[The sequence of appendices and photographs has been governed by the mechanical requirements of a book put together the way this one had to be. The pages should really be read in pairs: first the text pages, which demonstrate the fallacy of recent overdevelopment of the Colorado and the compounding error of new overdevelopment now being promoted; last, the photographs and text about what is gone and going.]   D. B.

RICHARD NORGAARD: *Approach to Music Temple, 1963*

DANIEL B. LUTEN: *Lake Powell rising on the same wall, June 1964 and 250 feet still to rise*

The waters impounded by this plug of artificial stone spread back through G Canyon . . . inundating the sparkling river, swallowing its luminous cliffs and tapestried walls, and extinguishing far into the long, dim, distant future everything that gave it life. As the waters into the side canyons, enveloping one by one their mirroring pools, drowning their bright flowers, backing up their clear, swe springs with stale flood water, a fine opa silt settles over all, covering rocks and trees alike with a gray slimy ooze. Darkness pervades the canyons. Death and the thickening, umbrageous gloom take over where life and shimmer light were the glory of the river.

ELIOT PORTER

ELIOT PORTER: Wall at entrance to Music Temple, 1962

We owe it to ourselves and to mankind to give full rein to our instinctive love of Natural Beauty, and to train and refine every inclination and capacity we have for appreciating it till we are able to see all those finer glories of which we now discover only the first faint glow.

SIR FRANCIS YOUNGHUSBAND

Drifting here, you learned to perceive, not to precon-
ceive, what makes a land beautiful. Beauty is where you
see it and you saw it often where the big river, thin-edged
with green, slid along under the pastel tapestries. An old
river had built the stone grain by grain, and the new river
was shaping it. You didn't quite catch the river in the
act of sculpturing, but the color of the Colorado assured
you that creation was still going on.

Down in the main gorge the vista was fine enough, but
what really counted was what you could seek out in a
hundred tributary clefts. You knew when the big boats
should be tied up and people should start walking, and
you learned to know Warm Springs, the silence of Moki
Canyon, and the strangeness of Hole-in-the-Rock. There
were the antiquities that you discovered, and some that
would never be.

DAVID BROWER: Clear Creek grasses

DAVID BROWER: Clear Creek ferns

RICHARD NORGAARD: *Plunge pool, Cathedral in the Dese*

There was somber color in places the desert sun never
knew. High above the noonday twilight you might have
looked small but you felt big. For all the massiveness and
height, your own good feet could put you there and had.
There was time to rest in shady silence, to wonder how,
to begin to understand why, once again, to know yourself.

DAVID BROWER: *Wall at entrance, Cathedral in the Desert*

RICHARD NORGAARD: *Plunge pool, Cathedral in the Desert*

Bridge Creek joined Aztec Creek, and Aztec and a
hundred others the Colorado, where a bank beaver had a
home but his progeny will not. For the flood has come
that does not recede and the natural world will miss what
the ages built here, and here alone. Just a few miles below
the junction the great dam is at work. Not to put water
on land. Not to control the river. Not to save water in an
arid land. But to divert the force that created beauty, to
generate kilowatt hours of electricity instead, while other
sources of energy lie idle. For a replaceable commodity we
spent this irreplaceable grandeur. Your son may pass close
to it. But neither he nor any man yet to be born will ever
again know it, nor will the intimate things that gave this
place its magic ever again know the sun.

RICHARD NORGAARD: Floor, Cathedral in the Desert

RICHARD NORGAARD: *Cathedral in the Desert*
Until June 1965; then Lake Powell

Remember these things lost; and under the vaulting
roof of the cathedral burn a candle to the memory.

Man always kills the thing he loves, and so we the pioneers have killed our wilderness. Some say we had to. Be that as it may, I am glad I shall never be young without wild country to be young in. Of what avail are forty freedoms without a blank spot on the map?

ALDO LEOPOLD

It is legitimate to hope that there may left . . . the special kind of human mark, the special record of human passage, that distinguishes man from all other species. It is rare enough among men, impossible to any other form of life. *It is simply the deliberate and chosen refusal to make any marks at all.* Sometimes we have withheld our power to destroy, and have left a threatened species like the buffalo, a threatened beauty spot like Yosemite or Yellowstone or Dinosaur, scrupulously alone. We are the most dangerous species of life on the planet, and every other species, even the earth itself, has cause to fear our power to exterminate. But we are also the only species which, when it chooses to do so, will go to great effort to save what it might destroy.

It is a better world with some buffalo left in it, a richer world with some gorgeous canyons unmarred by signboards, hot-dog stands, super highways, or high-tension lines, undrowned by power or irrigation reservoirs. If we preserved as parks only those places that have no economic possibilities, we would have no parks. And in the decades to come, it will not be only the buffalo and the trumpeter swan who need sanctuaries. Our own species is going to need them too.

It needs them now.

WALLACE STEGNER

Lithographed by Barnes Press, Inc.
New York City, N.Y.